Two Jobs, No Life

Two Jobs, No Life

Learning to Balance Work and Home

Dr. Peter Marshall

KEY PORTER BOOKS

National Library of Canada Cataloguing in Publication Data

Marshall, Peter, 1947-
    Two jobs, no life : learning to balance work and home

ISBN: 1-55263-365-9

1. Work and family. 2. Dual-career families. I. Title.

HD4904.25.M37 2001   646.7'0085   C2001-901683-2

THE CANADA COUNCIL | LE CONSEIL DES ARTS
FOR THE ARTS | DU CANADA
SINCE 1957 | DEPUIS 1957

ONTARIO ARTS COUNCIL
CONSEIL DES ARTS DE L'ONTARIO

The publisher gratefully acknowledges the support of the Canada Council for
the Arts and the Ontario Arts Council for its publishing program.

We acknowledge the financial support of the Government of Canada through
the Book Publishing Industry Development Program (BPIDP) for our publishing activities.

Key Porter Books Limited
70 The Esplanade
Toronto, Ontario
Canada M5E 1R2

www.keyporter.com

Portions of Chapter 6 have been previously published in Now I Know Why Tigers Eat
Their Young: Surviving a New Generation of Teenagers *(Whitecap, 2000). For more
information visit www.petermarshall.com.*

Electronic formatting: Jean Lightfoot Peters

Printed and bound in Canada

01 02 03 04 05 6 5 4 3 2 1

For my family—the best job I've ever had

Contents

8 Help on the Horizon:

Preface

Several months ago my son, Aaron, was completing an English assignment. He emerged from his bedroom to ask me for a definition of "irony." I did my best to oblige. A while later—and in a totally different context—he enquired why I appeared so harried. After all, it was the weekend and I was not relaxing like the rest of the family. I was forced to admit that I had not exactly been a joy to live with. In my own defense, however, I reminded him that I was in the middle of writing a book and lamented that the speed with which the deadline was approaching was awesome, while my rate of production was not. I pointed out that I still had to run the practice, do the grocery shopping, cook meals and put up with the fact that every time I sat down to write, someone or something interrupted me.

Aaron paused for a moment, then looking at me quizzically asked, "And what exactly is the book about?" Eager to get back to work—and somewhat impatient at yet another interruption—I reminded him that the book was about making sure you do not become too stressed by the demands of having both a job and a family. As he walked off, he remarked, "*Now* I understand the meaning of irony."

I have learned to accept that, while the goals I have for my life will not always be attained, they can at least give me a sense of direction and remind me of my priorities. Aaron's insight made me realize that I wrote this book as much for myself as for the reader. Although I have been a working parent for thirty-four years, I have yet to perfect the balance between work and home. I remain confident, however, that I can take many steps to come closer to effecting this balance—I am also convinced that the effort is worthwhile.

Let me introduce the other members of my family who will be mentioned from time to time. Joanne and Tim are our two adult children; Aaron and his younger sisters, Kiera and Alexandra, still live at home. Kathy—wife and mother—knows that I will never get the balance right and expects only my advance as compensation.

I also want to thank Kris Ongaro who helped prepare the manuscript and showed remarkable ability to cope with the stress I shamelessly introduced into our already busy practice.

Earlier this year Linda Sanders invited me to speak at the wellness fair she had organized for government employees. The fair reflected the growing awareness of the need to balance work and home. I asked if she would be kind enough to review parts of the manuscript. Her suggestions and comments were valuable and have been incorporated into the chapter on family-friendly work environments. Thank you, Linda.

Introduction:
The Balancing Act

Until recently, my high school history teacher was remembered as nothing more than living proof that the capacity to be boring and irrelevant was a marketable skill. Although I am sure he sensed our disdain for his subject, he persisted in his attempts to convince us of the importance of studying the past as a means of understanding the present and planning for the future. If I could remember his name I would publicly apologize for my failure to appreciate his wisdom. He was right—I did have an attitude problem.

One of the lessons I have learned from history is how natural it is for the relationship between work and home to change. Over the years this relationship has constantly evolved in order to adapt to society's broader trends and needs. Prior to the nineteenth century, for example, it was common for all members of the family to remain together throughout much of the day. Work and home were intertwined; cottage industries were common and the routine of the father leaving home in the morning to go to work was by no means standard.

Laura Ingalls Wilder's stories of pioneer life in the latter part of the nineteenth century became the basis of the long-running television series *Little House on the Prairie.* Her books illustrate how both genders—while having distinct roles—combined to create a skilled domestic workforce. There is an account of how everyone contributed to making clothes. The process started with shearing a sheep and ended with a ready-to-wear Sunday suit. That her family knew all the steps along the way amazes me. Although I could pick a sheep out of a lineup, I am not sure I could catch one, and I know for certain I would not have a clue what to do with it if I did. Pa and the boys, however, could raise, catch, and shear sheep with hardly a second thought, while Ma and the girls were known for their skills in spinning, dyeing, and weaving.

The development of commerce and industry during the nineteenth century brought profound changes to this pattern. A family's work became divided into two components—domestic duties and paid outside employment. Although home and work were now separated, gender boundaries removed the need to balance responsibilities. Each gender was assigned just one of the components—women ran the home while men populated the workforce.

This traditional nuclear family prevailed until the latter half of the twentieth century and was exemplified in the fifties sitcom *Leave It to Beaver.* Mom—alias June Cleaver—viewed housework as a privilege rather than a chore. Each morning she'd wave cheerily as husband Ward headed off to work, and sons Beaver and Wally left for school. Then something went terribly wrong. The sixties hit with full force. In the unwritten final episode, Wally grows his hair long, finds out where the sexual revolution is being held, and leaves home to sign up. Beaver cultivates little green plants in the backyard, listens to Bob Dylan and Pink Floyd, and heads out to meet his brother at Woodstock. Ward handles his midlife crisis by running off with his secretary. And June? She shakes her head in disbelief, declaring, "I'm out of here." When last heard of, she had returned to school to launch a career as a mining engineer.

Is Anyone Home?

The sixties led to many changes in both family life and the work-force. One of the more dramatic was the rapid increase in the number of people who had to balance the demands of work and home. Thanks to a number of factors, the full-time homemaker would quickly become a thing of the past. Economics played an important role. Today, the average two-parent family needs seventy weeks of paid employment a year to maintain its standard of living, an increase of over twenty hours since the fifties. Unless one parent is willing to put in a lot of overtime, breadwinning can no longer be seen as primarily a man's job—it has to be shared. This economic motivation does not reflect only a desire for more creature comforts and luxury items; wages in many sectors of the workforce have not kept pace with increases in the cost of living. As a result, the percentage of families who would be living below the poverty line if only one parent worked has increased; approximately two-thirds of mothers report that they need to work to avoid financial hardship.

I will discuss gender roles in a later chapter. For now, I would like only to highlight the growing presence of women in almost all areas of the workforce since the middle of the twentieth century. The need for women to occupy the positions vacated by men during the Second World War led many to decide not to return to being full-time homemakers. The feminist movement was an additional factor: traditional roles were portrayed as restrictive, and the view that women were ill-suited for many types of employment was challenged and gradually eroded. As more young women entered the workforce, higher education became important for both genders as it offered the means to move into more skilled areas of employment. This trend in education has largely obliterated the differences between the genders in academic achievement: girls today are just as likely to graduate from high school and obtain postsecondary diplomas and degrees as boys. The desire to apply their education and skills has prompted many women to see childbirth as a short-term break in their careers rather than a prelude to becoming a full-time homemaker. Surveys tell us that a woman's investment in her career does not lessen her commitment to family life. Both roles are typically high priority, adding to the importance of balancing them for maximum efficiency and satisfaction.

It's also worth mentioning the rise in divorce rates, which was paralleled by an exponential growth in the number of single parents, the majority of whom were employed. I spent seven years as a single parent; I have no major complaints, and like many single-parent families we developed a special closeness. We spent a great deal of time together. If I had to go shopping, the kids usually came. Not that taking two small children around a grocery store and trying to explain why a cart full of marshmallows, chocolate milk, and potato chips would not encompass the four major food groups was my idea of a good time; it was just that they were too young to be left on their own. But there were many occasions on which a second parent would have come in handy. I was pursuing a career that placed many demands on my time, and I often felt as if I was being forced to choose between work and home. The goal of balancing the two roles was fine, but there were days when I was convinced that part of the condition of being a single parent was to be permanently imbalanced.

The high demands on single parents are not necessarily relieved when they remarry, as almost all will do eventually. Most parents in stepfamilies are also employed and have the continuing demands of their work to balance with the added challenges of their new family. Speaking from personal experience again, these challenges begin as soon as the prospect of remarriage raises its head. It took many years to convince Kathy that marrying me and establishing a stepfamily with two adolescent children would be her ticket to perpetual bliss.

Staying Home and Living Longer

As a result of all these shifts and trends, the prevalence of the traditional nuclear family with a stay-at-home mother has declined rapidly; today, only 7 percent of families in North America conform to this model. The separation of roles into Ward and June Cleaver simplicity has diminished to the point where most adults in families are having to cope with the demands and pressures of both work and home.

What's more, this balancing act has become a long-term challenge. Family responsibilities are often extended far beyond our expectations. Children are remaining dependent for longer than was the case a few decades ago. When I was born, 50 percent of students left high school before graduating. Most found jobs and allowed their parents to become empty-nesters while the parents still had the energy to enjoy this boost to their mental health. The rate of graduation is now between 70 and 80 percent, and more young people are completing postsecondary education than ever before. Many also act as if leaving home before the age of thirty-five would be nothing short of wild and reckless. As a result, having a child and receiving a life sentence can seem like one and the same thing.

Family responsibilities are also prolonged if we find ourselves joining the "sandwich generation"—those men and women who are simultaneously caring for their children and parents. Issues relating to the sandwich generation will be the subject of a later chapter, but one frequent source of conflict and frustration is the extent to which work can interfere with providing care for elderly parents. This conflict often increases over time. Life expectancy is at an all-time high, but good health is far from guaranteed, and our parents can become increasingly dependent on us for their day-to-day needs.

The Good Old Days?

I must be careful not to overstate my case. While this balancing act can indeed be stressful and challenging, I do not believe it is a prelude to society's downfall. Each generation adapts in order to face its challenges, and the family is a highly resilient, resourceful, and adaptive institution. There are those, however, who would disagree. Dr. Benjamin Spock, who wrote the most successful child care book of all time, became sadly disillusioned with the trends in family life. Shortly before his death he lamented, "Tote it up and you have a picture of a society speeding downhill." Commenting on the near extinction of the stay-at-home parent and the abandonment of children to day care centers, a prominent child psychiatrist, Paul Steinhauer, recently predicted "disastrous results" for the next generation.

This tendency to view change as symptomatic of decline led to my interest in what I have called the Chicken Little Syndrome (CLS). For those of you who have not *yet* purchased my first book, *Now I Know Why Tigers Eat Their Young,* CLS is a complex disorder. (This is the heavy section of the chapter, but rest assured I cannot maintain a scholarly facade for more than a few lines.) At CLS's core is something I have labeled "sociological hypochondriasis." I picked this term because it meets the criteria for scientific respectability—it is totally incomprehensible and has more than five syllables per word. Like the physical hypochondriac, for whom a mere twinge is sufficient cause to summon friends and loved ones to his bedside, the sociological hypochondriac looks at what is happening in society and immediately sees signs of decay and imminent disaster.

Many afflicted with CLS also have a severe case of the GOD (Good Old Days) complex. They, too, look at the demise of the stay-at-home mother with utter dismay, convinced that we need to return to a wonderful bygone era when the quality of family life was much higher. This assumption that the Cleaver model should be the gold standard against which all other forms of family life are judged is, however, questionable. For example, some have argued that the increase in divorce was more a *response* to problems in family life than a cause of them. The GOD notion also ignores the fact that society constantly evolves. The old model of family life and its relationship to the workforce existed because it met the needs of society at that particular point in history. But the world changed. To my mind, there is little point evaluating current models by comparing them to those that existed in the past. It is far more productive to focus on how we can make our present-day lifestyle as successful as possible. This book's goal is to make a small contribution to this process. After reviewing the many factors that contribute to work-family conflict, I discuss the continuing impact of gender stereotyping on family life. Given my belief that parents rarely pay sufficient attention to their own needs, *two* chapters are devoted to how we can take better care of ourselves. Fully relaxed and re-energized, the reader can then move on to chapters relating to how we take care of the important people in our lives—our children and our aging parents. This is followed by a discussion of the recent trends in making the workplace more "family-friendly." I end with a topic that has become of great interest to me in my work as a psychologist—determining the factors that make families resilient and capable of adapting to the constant change in society. You will find quizzes, questionnaires, and checklists throughout the book. They can be fun to complete; they can also be a way to help you recognize and overcome the sources of work-family conflict.

1 | Two Jobs—No Life?

So here we are in the early days of the twenty-first century. Ward and June Cleaver are a thing of the past, and I am not sure too many of us even care. But while we enjoy our careers and our families, the hectic pace of our day-to-day lives—making lunches, school drop-offs, commuting, playtime—can leave us feeling ragged. When we stop to think about it, we may realize that this juggling act has left us with two jobs—work and home—and not much of a life.

Multiple Roles and the Spillover Effect

Juggling multiple roles is part of everyday life. Most of the time we move from one role to another without even thinking. After a while, it comes naturally and doesn't feel like "juggling" at all. Writing this chapter prompted me to count the number of roles I have assumed this morning. It is just before 10 a.m. and the count is already at six. It started with "author"—getting up at 4 a.m. is not easy, but it does guarantee a couple of hours' peace and quiet. By 6:30 a.m. the fact that three of our children still live with us could no longer be denied, and I moved into the "parent" role. This was followed by "spouse" as Kathy and I had a quick cabinet meeting to organize the day and coordinate schedules (it never works, but we feel good about trying). A brief call to a friend and a stop by the office added two more roles. I slipped into the "customer" mode long enough to get the dry cleaning and a large cup of coffee before heading home to resume being an author.

Social psychologists tell us that it is common for people to have more than ten roles—up to sixteen is not uncommon. Some are major, such as spouse, parent, and employee. Others are less central in our lives; being the assistant coach on a children's soccer team or a volunteer canvasser are possible examples. Roles can also be distinguished on the basis of their importance to our self-concept or by the required investment of time and effort. The degree of importance and the level of investment may be similar, but this is not always the case. For example, my role as a brother is very important to me, although the investment of time and effort is relatively low given the geographical distance between us.

The fact that we have to juggle many roles is not, of itself, a problem. To the contrary, the research tells us that the more roles we have, the more satisfying our lives are likely to be. We have greater opportunity to experience a sense of achievement and less opportunity to get bored. We meet more people and broaden our social support network.

The value of maintaining many roles in our lives is relevant for understanding the relationship between work and home. The terms "positive spillover" and "enhancement" have been used to describe how this relationship can, in fact, be beneficial. Positive experiences in one area "spill over" into the other and contribute to the person's overall feelings of satisfaction and achievement. Although this finding applies to both genders, some of the studies involving only women are particularly convincing. One tracked a large group of women for eighteen years. Those who were employed and had children at home had the lowest mortality rate.

Negative spillover can also occur. Work and home are usually the areas of our lives that are the most demanding in terms of time and energy. Several studies have found that difficulty balancing these two roles is the number-one source of stress for employed parents with children living at home. Even if it were feasible, relinquishing one of the roles would probably not be an acceptable solution. We all have days when we feel like quitting our jobs or heading out for a loaf of bread and never coming back. The main reason we do not act on such impulses is that so much of our self-concept and emotional life is invested in our work and family roles. We pride ourselves on being good employees; we pride ourselves on being good parents. Organizing our lives so that the relationship between these roles is one of peaceful co-existence rather than competition and conflict is, therefore, an important but sometimes very challenging goal.

Understanding Stress

Before considering the complex relationship between work and home, I would like to talk more generally about stress. Estimates vary, but costs resulting from stress run into many billions of dollars each year. These costs take into account both health care and the lowered workplace productivity that results from decreased efficiency and stress-related absence. Approximately 25 percent of the adult population complain of recurrent fatigue; among those who seek help from their family doctor, less than 10 percent will be diagnosed with an underlying physical cause. For the remainder, chronic stress is the most likely culprit. Learning how to recognize and monitor stress offers a way to avoid reaching the stage where you are becoming overloaded and heading towards burnout.

Stress, like cholesterol, comes in good and bad forms. At times it can be hard to tell the difference; the good can turn into the bad (or even the downright ugly) without the person recognizing what is happening. The transition from good to bad is illustrated by the four stages of stress:

Stage 1 stress can be really good for you. It fires up your enthusiasm and motivation. Psychologists have used the phrase "optimal level of arousal" to refer to the fact that a certain level of stress is beneficial when it comes to performing tasks. The extremes, however, decrease efficiency. The low end of the stress dimension verges on vegetative and is exemplified by a child's response to being asked to do chores. In this case, your chances of detecting signs of optimal arousal are minimal and the only discernible stress is yours. The other end of the dimension also leads to poor performance. Even when people are highly motivated to do well, very high levels of stress interfere with their ability to do so. The brain resembles an overheated engine—still running, but not at maximum efficiency and at risk of stalling if not given a chance to cool down.

During Stage 1 you are still enjoying the benefits of optimal, mid-range stress. You are doing well, but as paradoxical as it might seem, this may not be good.

Stage 2 is where you begin to become a victim of your own success. Stress can be seductive. The positive effects noted for Stage 1 create a certain risk. Success tends to be rewarded with the expectation that you can take on more work and responsibility. Your reputation as a competent and energetic person will precede you, and you are likely to be the first one honored with a new responsibility or task. Initially, you're flattered. Over time, however, you begin to feel punished and overburdened. Your energy level decreases, and your feelings of control and accomplishment give way to fatigue and tension. The end result can be an escalating level of stress that becomes increasingly detrimental.

The hallmark of *Stage 3* stress is its self-defeating quality. Due to rising feelings of resentment, you start to act in ways that make matters a lot worse. You are no longer flattered when new assignments and responsibilities come your way. To the contrary, you now feel that you are being treated unfairly. Employers are seen as unreasonable and demanding taskmasters, and resentment towards other employees can develop. In your eyes, they are not pulling their weight, yet they're getting the same pay for work of much less value. Relationships deteriorate. You become irritable and snappy—even downright miserable—and begin to isolate yourself. Your behavior can also prompt others to avoid you. The first choice of a companion at break time is unlikely to be the person who is irritable, snappy, and downright miserable.

The self-defeating aspect of Stage 3 is that you begin to lose the social support that is such an important part of coping with day-to-day issues and problems. A situation is created in which you damage relationships just when they are needed most.

There are, of course, work situations in which people are quite isolated from one another; there are also times when a particular work environment is far from supportive. For the majority of employees, however, relationships at work are a valued part of their social world. These relationships serve many purposes. One is to support people in completing the job itself; fellow employees give and ask for advice and generally help each other out. But they also get to know one another at a more personal level, and it would be a strange workplace in which the conversation involved only lively discussions about company philosophy and the policies and procedures manual. Movies, sports, vacations, and the sorry state of the world and one's children are far more likely.

All of the elements of the three stages can apply to the home just as readily as they do to the workplace. As will be discussed in the next chapter, the "Superwoman myth" has been particularly seductive, creating the expectation that women can, and therefore should, maintain a cheery smile and sunny disposition in their role as the primary parent and housekeeper in spite of the fact that they have demanding jobs. More generally, members of the family can feel that other people are not pulling their weight and, in the absence of attempts to rectify the situation, resentment can become chronic. Angry, irritable people are no more fun to be around at home than they are at work, and relationships, together with the support they bring, deteriorate.

During *Stage 4* the inability to cope with the demands of life becomes obvious to all concerned. Depression, addiction, and an array of mental health difficulties can all occur. Chronically high stress has been related to a threefold increase in the risk of early death, as well as heightened susceptibility to cardiovascular disease, hypertension, cancer, and musculoskeletal disorders. It can also have a devastating impact on relationships and is one factor contributing to the high rate of divorce.

If you are fortunate enough to be permanently stuck in Stage 1, return this book to me for a full refund, enclosing your secret so that I can sell it to others for vast sums. Otherwise, please read on.

When Roles Collide

As much as the idea of "enhancement" has its appeal, "scarcity" cannot be ignored when considering both stress and the relationship between work and home. The idea is straightforward—a person has only so much energy to go around. Multiple roles that might, of themselves, be very important and rewarding are now competing for these resources, creating high levels of stress.

Two types of conflict between work and home have been described. One results from the feeling that the demands of family life are encroaching on work, making it hard to do a good job. These demands can be general—financial problems, for example, or feeling chronically stretched for time. They can also be more specific, such as marital conflict or coping with a sick child. The second type of conflict occurs when work is the problem—due either to the demands of the job itself, or poor relationships with co-workers. Whatever the cause, pressure and stress from work spills over, and life at home suffers. The situation becomes particularly hard to manage when both types of conflict exist at the same time. "Bidirectional negative spillover" sounds nasty—and it is. Two roles that are supposed to be rewarding and satisfying collide and take a lot of the joy out of life.

Tammy Allen, a researcher at the University of South Florida, reviewed the many studies in this area. More than 80 percent of women report some degree of work-family conflict; the figure is lower for men but still exceeds 70 percent. As for the impact of this conflict, a threefold increase in the incidence of mood disorders such as depression has been found among people who report that the pressures of their jobs interfere with their family lives. When the demands of people's home lives intruded into the workplace, however, the increase was *thirtyfold*. Anxiety and substance abuse are also more common; again, this is particularly the case for people who find that their home lives are undermining their efficiency at work.

Why is the stress that occurs when home interferes with work more detrimental than the reverse situation? One reason could be availability of that most useful of defense mechanisms—rationalization. Although I hope I accept at least some responsibility for what goes wrong in my life, the opportunity to blame someone else is hard to pass up—why add guilt and self-reproach to your list of woes? Many work environments provide ample opportunity to hold others responsible when the pressures of the job lead to negative spillover. A lack of adequate staff, a flood of work orders that came out of nowhere, and a supervisor who is incapable of distinguishing between fair labor practices and slavery are all potential targets for blame, often with at least some justification. At home, *we* are the "management." We brought the children into the world, and we are supposed to be able to make family life successful. When problems occur, the blame is ours, as is the responsibility for the negative impact on work. This powerful combination of guilt and stress can have particularly negative effects on a person's well-being.

Research has confirmed that the conflict between work and home is the cause, rather than a consequence, of problems such as depression and substance abuse. One study by Michael Frone and his colleagues at the Research Institute on Addictions in New York tracked almost three hundred employed parents for four years. A steady increase in the conflict between work and home led to the eventual onset of stress-related disorders.

I once read an article about the negative impact of work-home conflict on air traffic controllers. What made the experience memorable was that I was on a flight from North Carolina to Toronto at the time. My immediate impulse was to ask the pilot to radio ahead and casually ask our controller how things were going at work and slip in few questions about his life at home. Recognizing that my plan was seriously flawed, I read on. I was greatly relieved to learn that air traffic controllers are able to tolerate high levels of stress at work; the spillover is likely to occur at home, not in the control tower. Their interactions with their children can become less sensitive and responsive. Marital conflict also tends to increase, which often has a more noticeable effect on a woman's mental health. Although the reason for this gender difference is not clear, it probably reflects the persistent cultural view that women are primarily responsible for family life. Other studies have looked at the effect of spillover on sexual relationships. When the stress associated with work-family conflict leads to fatigue, passions are dampened, if not temporarily extinguished.

Returning to Allen's review, the range of problems associated with work-family conflict is broad and has been documented for many different occupational groups, including nurses, retail workers, navy personnel, teachers, restaurant staff, small business owners, accountants, and real estate agents. Based on the major findings from studies around the world, she concluded that "work-family conflict has costly effects on individual work life, home life, and general well-being and health."

How Do You Rate?

Psychologists have scales for absolutely everything. I know of least three that measure loneliness in Zimbabwe (I am not making this up), and the Turkish version of a questionnaire to measure habitual thinking made it into the *Journal of Personality Assessment.* Although we go overboard at times, quantifying aspects of human experience can be useful. It provides a way of measuring change, and may also help pinpoint specific areas of strength and difficulty. This type of self-monitoring is valuable in recognizing the signs of excessive stress. With this in mind, I invite you to complete a questionnaire designed to measure work-family conflict. When you are finished, tally your score. A score of 48 or below means you are to be envied; you are perfectly balanced and now have the data to prove it. The higher you climb above 48, the more stress you are likely to be experiencing. A score of around 90 is not uncommon among people in the workshops I have given; many score higher.

Work-Family Conflict Scale

Items are answered on the following 5-point scale: 1, strongly disagree; 2, disagree; 3, neither agree nor disagree; 4, agree; 5, strongly agree.

1.	My job keeps me away from my family too much.	1	2	3	4	5
2.	I feel I have more to do than I can handle comfortably.	1	2	3	4	5
3.	I do not have a good balance between my job and my family time.	1	2	3	4	5
4.	I wish I had more time to do things for my family.	1	2	3	4	5
5.	I feel physically drained when I get home from work.	1	2	3	4	5
6.	I feel emotionally drained when I get home from work.	1	2	3	4	5
7.	I feel I have to rush to get everything done each day.	1	2	3	4	5

8. My time off from work does not match other family members' schedules well.

   1   2   3   4   5

9. I feel I don't have enough time for myself.

   1   2   3   4   5

10. I worry that other people at work think my family interferes with my job.

   1   2   3   4   5

11. I worry whether I should work less and spend more time with my children.

   1   2   3   4   5

12. I do not find enough time for my children.

   1   2   3   4   5

13. I worry about how my kids are when I'm working.

   1   2   3   4   5

14. I am not comfortable with the arrangements for my children while I am working.

   1   2   3   4   5

15. Making arrangements for my children while I work involves a lot of effort.

   1   2   3   4   5

16. I worry that other people feel I should spend more time with my children.

   1   2   3   4   5

17. My work schedule often conflicts with my family life.

   1   2   3   4   5

	1	2	3	4	5
18. After work, I come home too tired to do some of the things I'd like to do.	1	2	3	4	5
19. On the job, I have so much work that it takes away from my other interests.	1	2	3	4	5
20. My family dislikes how often I am preoccupied with my work while I'm at home.	1	2	3	4	5
21. Because my work is demanding, at times I am irritable at home.	1	2	3	4	5
22. The demands of my job make it difficult to be relaxed all the time at home.	1	2	3	4	5
23. My work takes up time that I'd like to spend with my family.	1	2	3	4	5
24. My job makes it difficult to be the kind of spouse or parent that I'd like to be.	1	2	3	4	5

I would like to end on a note of optimism—in spite of the fact that I have presented a long list of the trials and tribulations awaiting those who feel that the relationship between work and home is one of running warfare. If you are such a person, please accept my assurance that the situation is not hopeless. There are many approaches to preventing or reducing the stress that the work-home conflict can generate. These will be discussed in subsequent chapters, and the chances are good that you will survive long enough to read them. Being aware of the pitfalls and evaluating your level of risk, however, are valuable first steps. "Know your enemy" is a very applicable maxim; the more you recognize what might happen, the easier it is to protect yourself.

Superwoman and Mr. Mom

I grew up in an era when "gender stereotyping" was a way of life rather than a problem. By the time I was nine, I knew I was destined to be something manly like a fireman, farmer, or fighter pilot—florist was out. My wife would stay home with the kids. Such was the script, and no one I knew talked about a rewrite. Things eventually changed, but not in a balanced way; women's roles were revised dramatically, men's were not. Many women were no longer willing to accept that their major areas of achievement should be confined to hearth and home. Success in education and employment became important goals and provided opportunities for power and influence that would never be attainable if they remained dependent on their husbands. As a result, women entered the workforce in droves. Men, however, were not voicing too many complaints about their lot in life, nor were they insisting on equal opportunity in the kitchen or nursery.

In spite of their entry into the workforce, women never lessened their commitment to their families. Surveys indicate that both work and home receive the highest priority ratings from women. But as important as these two roles may be, women often place expectations on themselves that become excessive and render them especially vulnerable to becoming overwhelmed and depressed. Even when partnered with an able-bodied spouse, women continue to assume most of the responsibility for child care and housework. This inequity remains regardless of the number of hours women are employed and can be found in many countries; women all over the industrialized world work longer hours than men when both paid employment and domestic responsibilities are taken into consideration. This difference exists before children are born but reaches a peak when there are infants and preschool children in the family.

I doubt you will be surprised to hear that surveys reveal men are far less concerned about the inequitable division of labor than women. It could be that we are callous creatures with the emotional intelligence and sensitivity of molluscs. I would rather defer this diagnosis and take a brief excursion into history to argue that both women and men are, in some ways, victims of many years of relentless stereotyping. The idea that men are victims may be a hard sell, but I like challenges.

A Woman's Place

During the industrial revolution a woman's job description was fairly straightforward—raise a generation of hard-working citizens who will meet the growing need for skilled workers. With infant mortality high, and life expectancy much lower than it is today, women had to devote most of their adult lives to this task. The experts of the day were highly creative and versatile in their efforts to convince women to accept such a role. Some used the "aren't you so lucky to be home with the eleven kids all day" approach. The popular *Glaxo Baby Book* of the Victorian era assured the mother that "ten thousand raptures thrill her bosom" as she tended to her baby. Complaints were not to be voiced or even expected; given her exalted role, a mother's gratitude was supposed to increase with each new load of laundry and sink full of dishes. After all, in the 1897 manual, *What a Young Man Should Know*, Sylvanus Stall had observed that "an idle woman is always an unhappy woman. Her household duties are no misfortune, but a blessing." The fact that he had presumably never been blessed did not seem to deter him from adding that domestic activities would awaken "that which is noblest and best in a woman's nature," and bring her happiness, health, and long life. Another writer added allure to this list of benefits, pronouncing that the mother "never looks so charming as when she is attending to her household duties."

If the mother who was confronted with a double-digit progeny but none of the advantages of indoor plumbing and morning cartoons was beginning to tire of waiting for that first rapture, she could at least expect ample reward in the afterlife. The Victorian author and child care expert Lydia Child seemed to make no distinction between motherhood and paradise. She commented, "Does not the little cherub in his way guide you to heaven, marking the pathway by the flowers as he goes?" "No" would have been my guess, but perhaps too many years of child-rearing have left me jaded. In a similar vein, I wonder if my wife and I have set our sights too low when it comes to our expectations of the rewards that will be ours once the children are grown up and able to repay us for our years of selfless devotion. I suspect Kathy would happily settle for the occasional invitation at Christmas, a collect call on Mother's Day, and the experience of watching them voluntarily hang up their coats when they visit. This pales in comparison to the promise that children will grow up to "revere you and be the solace of your declining years."

I am not sure too many women were convinced. But if the incentives did not motivate them, guilt could be relied on to do the job. Guilt is one of the best motivators—and it can be more powerful than legislation when it comes to influencing behavior. We sometimes dismiss laws as external rules that can be ignored without so much as a hint of remorse. Just think of the ease with which people look a custom's officer in the eye and insist that they really did need two bulging suitcases for their personal clothing and only purchased a few inexpensive souvenirs for the kids. By way of contrast, the unwritten rules that form part of our socialization can remain influential throughout our lives; intellectually we may decide that the rule is unnecessary or even silly, but emotionally we know guilt will be unavoidable if we break it.

Historically, the power of guilt to control behavior has been tremendously effective as a way of enforcing gender boundaries. Let me emphasize that there was no evil intent; the goal was to maintain a pattern of family life that best met the needs of society. As long as a child was deemed a success story, the mother could expect to be given full credit. But if her little cherub ended up scattering thistles instead of flowers upon the pathways of life, she had no one to blame but herself. The noted child care expert of the day, John Abbott, insisted that the mother was the sole determinant of the child's personality and behavior. He pointed to the alarming number of "lunatics, dissolutes, and vile adults" who were the direct result of poor mothering. If she failed in her duty, she was condemned to eternal guilt. Even if she somehow managed to slip into heaven, her children would drop by to haunt her on their way to the place set aside for those who have spent their time on earth as dissolutes, lunatics, and otherwise vile adults. The scene was horrific: "When you meet your children at the bar of God and they point to you and say, 'It was your neglect of duty which banished us from Heaven and consigned us to endless woe,' you must feel what no tongue can tell. Oh, it is dreadful for a mother to trifle with duty. Eternal destinies are committed to your trust."

If a guilty conscience wasn't enough to keep mom's feet firmly placed in the nursery, the education system was certainly willing to help the cause. The assumption that boys were destined to work outside the home made them obvious candidates for an education that could prepare them for competitive employment. But girls were a different story. As pronounced by John Gregory in his popular book *A Father's Legacy to His Daughters*, education for girls was "an enemy to delicacy." If they had managed to learn anything deeper than the best way to get rid of ring-around-the-collar, they were to keep it to themselves: "If you happen to have any learning, keep it a profound secret, especially from men" was the advice. If such advice seemed unpalatable, you were reminded that the Virgin Mary—the undisputed role model for any girl—"knew nothing of letters." The fact that Joseph might not have scored too well on reading or spelling tests was conveniently ignored. For the more enlightened, some degree of education for women was acceptable but should not extend beyond subjects such as literature, history, and geography.

Biological theories were also put forward to ensure that women would not want to venture from the home. Higher education would cause atrophy of the uterus by diverting the body's energy to the brain, and the breasts would cease to be operational. One prominent obstetrician declared with confidence that Euclidian geometry was the most damaging when it came to inhibiting development of the mammary glands. If fear of physical damage did not suffice, the threat of insanity loomed. Proof was offered: women in asylums were more likely to be educated than were male patients. The brainwork had simply been too much for their feeble minds.

In the face of the arguments used to maintain gender role stereotyping, it was inevitable that the movement towards equal opportunity in the workforce would be prolonged and arduous. No one disputed the role of the biological distinctions between the genders; what was criticized by early feminists, however, was the prejudice and pigeon-holing that accompanied them. In 1866, Emily Davies remarked, "It is not against the recognition of real distinction, but against arbitrary judgements not based on reason that the protest is made." This protest continues to be necessary; more than a century later, researchers continue to find that, although the techniques might be more subtle, boys receive more reinforcement for learning than girls. Only very recently have young women demonstrated that they can easily hold their own in applied sciences such as engineering while somehow retaining their figures and fertility.

Has Anyone Seen Dad?

Not long ago someone in desperate need of a Ph.D. came up with the idea of recording how much time fathers spend with their infant children. The average time was apparently under three minutes a day, which I doubt impressed the subjects' spouses. There are many indications that we have come a long way since then. More recent surveys tell us that most men far exceed the three-minute time limit and are more willing to become involved in all aspects of parenting. Some share parental leave with their partners, and there are even websites for stay-at-home fathers. At the same time, however, gender role stereotypes continue to exert an influence. While women have been highly motivated to enter areas that were previously male-dominated, men seem far more reluctant to cross traditional gender lines and involve themselves in all aspects of family life.

The traditional model of family life had appointed the father as head of the household. In principle, this lofty position allowed men to have a great deal of influence over child-rearing and other aspects of family life. But the concept of "role centrality" needs to be taken into consideration. People put the most time and effort into roles that are central to their self-esteem and feelings of well-being. Society's traditional division of labor taught men to view their working lives as central. As a result, their self-esteem was, and often remains, closely tied to success in their careers. Raising the children and taking care of the house were not central and were, therefore, delegated to women.

Early writers in the child care field also assumed that whatever time men spent in the home would be devoted to pursuits that had nothing to do with children. Manuals for husbands were more likely to espouse the merits of letter-writing, keeping a journal, and novel-reading than give advice about fatherhood. There was the occasional voice urging men to see the merits and benefits of parenthood. Dr. Stall's manual gave center stage to mothers in the home but decreed "it is not only the father's duty, but it ought also to be his pleasure to look after his own children." He argued that fathers should see the baby as a blessing and that the "little woman" could not, and should not, do it all. Anticipating some resistance, he addressed the inhibitions that fathers needed to overcome, reassuring them that they could still be real men even if spied by friends and neighbors wheeling the baby carriage in the park.

But advice of this nature was the exception. Child care literature throughout most of the last century reinforced the view that mothers were, in effect, single parents. Authors of textbooks in child psychology were often of a similar mind. A popular series in the 1960s made almost one hundred references to the mother's role in development. Dad made one appearance, but only in reference to research with families of macaque monkeys. Society's view that a man's influence and success were to be judged primarily by his performance in the workplace remained largely unchallenged.

The Continuing Legacy: The Superwoman Myth

The persistence of these gender boundaries has created problems—particularly for women who decided to seek employment. The demands of work and home can be excessive, and the roles are often in conflict. Lynn Polasky and Carole Holahan, researchers at the University of Texas, studied the strategies used by women to cope with work-family conflict. Some had redefined their roles, adjusting their level of importance or centrality. An example of applying this strategy would be to "decentralize" the domestic role. The children still get fed and the standard of housekeeping remains above the contamination level. However, you decide that your level of involvement in this role will not be the same as would be possible for a full-time homemaker.

More common than redefinition, however, were attempts to conform to the "Superwoman myth"—the idea that women should be able to retain their traditional responsibilities in the home despite the fact that they had full-time jobs.

Physiological studies of stress speak to the reality of the "second shift" for women—they are never off duty. The level of stress-related hormones such as norepinephrine follows a distinct gender pattern. For a man, it is low first thing in the morning and often does not climb much higher until heading off to work. It falls steadily as he returns home and will stay low during his days off. The pattern is very different for a woman. It tends to jump rather than climb as she hops out of bed to get herself and the children ready for the day. It is high throughout the time she is at work, and remains so after she returns home to catch up on housework, help with homework, and get the children ready for bed. Days off do not really exist; stress levels often do not come down. This does not necessarily mean that her husband has reached an all-time norepinephrine low as he sinks into his arm-chair with a beer and the channel changer. He could be up and about, but he has probably taken on tasks that he sees as discretionary and manly. He is building a deck, painting the garage, or taking the children to their hockey game. His wife, on the other hand, is stuck with the day-to-day chores that no one likes. Among the list of "did we really need to know statistics" is the finding that 65 percent of such chores have to be done again the next day. Apart from the sheer drudgery this injects into daily life, the fact that the work is not seen as discretionary adds to the potential for stress; satisfaction with a task tends to increase the more we feel we have choice about its completion.

The differences in how women and men spend their time were documented by Reed Larsen and his colleagues at the University of Illinois. The subjects in their study were given a pager with the understanding they could be contacted randomly during their waking hours. When called, they would report what they were doing and how they felt about doing it. The material from this "day in the life of" study was not exactly enthralling, but it was reassuring to find that the subjects' lives were about as exciting and noteworthy as my own. As expected, women were far more involved in child care and housework. Moreover, they were less likely to find their home lives satisfying and relaxing. In fact, many derived far more enjoyment from their activities at work, especially if they had good relationships with fellow employees.

Those trapped in the Superwoman role are rarely content to remain there. They would willingly job share, but even if they have a partner, recruitment can be challenging. Most men in dual-earner families will state publicly that they believe family responsibilities should be shared. But, as my mother commented to me many times during my teenage years, "the path to hell is paved with good intentions." In fairness to my gender, the number of men who are actively involved in the full range of domestic activities is increasing. At the same time, discontent arising from inequitable distribution of labor in the home is currently one of the major causes of marital conflict; it is also linked to the higher incidence of depression among women.

Much depends on the expectations women have before they establish their families. Those who have more traditional views regarding gender roles are unlikely to be upset when childbirth adds substantially to their workload while hardly making a dent in their partner's leisure time. The number of women who hold this view, however, is relatively small. The majority expect job sharing at home and are far from content to find that they have a "sleeping partner" when it comes to most day-to-day aspects of domestic life.

Changing Times: Mr. Mom

I never thought to question the separation of roles when I first married; neither did my wife. I almost shudder when recalling the events surrounding my first son's birth. I was attending classes that day. My mother called to break the news and took me out to supper to celebrate, after which I stopped by the hospital to visit mom and baby. I next met Tim when he was discharged a few days later. The idea that men might have a role in pregnancy and childbirth had not yet entered our consciousness, and I cannot imagine what the reaction would have been had I suggested being present in the delivery room. By the time I remarried, my views regarding my role as a father had changed. I had been a single parent for many years and had discovered that young children are really not alien creatures. Attending prenatal classes was a given, although I still struggle to understand why I had to lie on the mat next to Kathy and pretend that all those breathing exercises would add to my repertoire of life skills. I count the births of Aaron, Kiera, and Alexandra among the most cherished moments of my life and, while I was spared the trials of delivery, I became no stranger to the day-to-day demands of colicky, pungent, and otherwise-in-need-of-attention infants.

My experiences are by no means unusual. Numerous studies have confirmed that fathers are becoming increasingly involved in child care. By the middle of the nineties, studies were emerging that indicated no difference between a mother's and father's commitment to raising children; one study even reported that fathers were just as anxious as mothers about their child's first day at nursery school. I am not aware of any research suggesting that men have developed greater enthusiasm for housework, but they are doing more of it. Their share had increased to approximately one-third by the mid-nineties.

Trends do not, of course, relate to everyone. The distant, peripheral father who needs his children to wear name tags still exists. While many fathers can feed and change a baby with the best of them, others believe there is nothing for them to do until junior is old enough to swing a baseball bat. As is the case for women, attitudes towards gender roles play an important part in determining who conforms to the trend. Fathers who have more egalitarian attitudes are more likely to be actively involved in all aspects of family life. They do not see their wives' employment as a dereliction of duty; paid employment, raising the children, and housework are all shared.

A number of other factors also have an impact on the nature of fathers' involvement with their children. The gender of the child has an influence. Although many fathers are active in caring for their daughters, this is more likely to be the case with sons. Age is another factor. When there is more than one child, mothers tend to focus on the younger children, especially infants, while fathers take the older children under their wings.

As much as gender stereotypes may have benefited men, there are ways in which they have been limiting and restrictive. Women who have jobs and children typically rate both as their highest priorities. Women are onto something. They wanted the best of both worlds and in order to achieve this goal, they expanded their job descriptions. Cutting back was not an option—no one advocated taking "caring" and "nurturing" off the list. Men, on the other hand, are taking longer to figure out that their lives will be also enriched if they expand their job descriptions. I hasten to add that I am not trying to paint an idyllic picture of the homemaker's day-to-day life. I have served my time in the trenches, and the fact that I no longer have any nose to wipe, other than my own, brings no great sadness. But I challenge you to name something more rewarding than holding your smiling child while he falls asleep in your arms or watching your daughter beam with pride and pleasure as she performs in a school concert.

One incentive for men to share domestic responsibilities is the realization of how important a role they can have in their children's lives. Contrary to notions that still appear in parenting literature, fathers are not limited to rough-and-tumble play and teaching instrumental skills. Observations of parent-child interactions demonstrate that fathers can be just as nurturing as mothers; they are equally responsive to their infants' vocalizations and movements and respond just as quickly to a baby's signs of distress. Acceptance of "nurturing" as a manly trait, however, is far from complete; while a recent article was optimistic that gender roles were becoming more equitable, it also referred to the characteristic predicting men's active involvement in child care as "feminism."

Earlier this year Wade Mackey at the University of Arkansas published an analysis of 55,000 observations of children's interactions with adults in twenty-three countries including Peru, Israel, the United States, India, Sri Lanka, Iceland, Morocco, Ivory Coast, and China. The observations were undertaken in sites such as parks, festivals, shopping areas, and workplaces. Mackey concluded that, when alone with their children, men's behavior was comparable to that observed for mothers in terms of the level of support, intimacy, and nurturing. He spoke of the "independent man-to-child-affiliative bond," which is a scholar's way of saying that men have got what it takes to be a parent in every sense of the word—they just may not use it yet.

In his recent article, *The New Psychology of Men,* Harvard's Ronald Levant talks of the damage caused when fathers are emotionally unavailable. Children are burdened with a feeling that they never knew their fathers; they never knew how their fathers felt or even if they liked and approved of them. A few years ago, I had an experience that poignantly illustrated this feeling of loss. The chance encounter led to the following broadcast on CBC's *First Person Singular:*

I had not anticipated a memorable experience as we waited for our order to arrive at Swiss Chalet. My daughter and I had been following the bus from her sister's skating tournament, but through a series of missed turns and faulty assumptions we found ourselves at the wrong restaurant. Realizing that scouring the city in search of our party was probably pointless, I resigned myself to the fact that I had lost the opportunity to have lunch with fifty or so pre-adolescent, pumped-up-for-the-competition, girls. My grief was manageable.

Alexandra loves to play cards, and almost as if prepared for this eventuality, she happened to have a deck in her pocket. We were beginning the first of a long series of hands when two middle-aged men walked over to our section. They were immersed in a conversation that was obviously so important to them that they did not pause or interrupt the flow as they sat down and settled themselves into the adjacent booth. Now, I like to think that I am a reasonably well brought up individual who knows better than to listen to other people's conversations, but I soon found myself straining to hear their every word. From their manner and way of talking to one another, I would guess they were not close friends but had stumbled across a topic that both needed to discuss—their fathers.

I wish I had heard the entire dialog, but unfortunately one had a rather quiet voice. Although I had already violated my code of social ethics, I could not bring myself to ask him to speak up. His companion, on the other hand, had one of those voices that, while not loud, was clear and carried well.

His father, it seemed, had died several years ago. He had been a provider, a husband, and a good parent to the children, and one of these attributes was a typical preface to the man's complaints. Perhaps "complaints" is too harsh—he didn't seem to feel that he had been treated badly. He was simply trying to understand why his father had been so hard to know. I don't think he realized they were strangers until well into his adult life. This insight had been as serendipitous as my finding myself his uninvited audience. There had been an unexpected telephone conversation with an uncle in Montreal, and in that four-minute exchange he felt he had discovered more about his father than he had learned throughout their entire time together. This experience made him aware of how their relationship had never progressed beyond the necessary and the superficial. He remembered that there had been times when he had wanted his father to really talk to him—even share his feelings. But this never happened. His father shared little, and the only emotion he expressed openly was an occasional outburst of anger. His companion's expressions told me that he identified with everything that was being said. There were no breaks in the conversation, and they looked intently at one another as if to offer support and understanding.

I doubt that the man had lived with his father for the last thirty years, but he seemed to long for an intimacy that had never been achieved. I wondered why the history of their relationship was so important to him now—it was as if he were still asking his father to become a person and not just a family figure. I tried to imagine the questions he would want to ask his father if he had the opportunity. But would he ask them, and how could the answers satisfy more than a certain curiosity? For people who know one another intimately, talking about things that matter is a habit, not an isolated, bare-it-all event.

I lost the series quite badly. Alexandra beamed as she packed up the cards, and we turned our attention to having lunch together. This had to meet the criteria for that hallmark of good parenting—quality time. Wasn't I adding to a store of memories that would guarantee my lifelong status as an involved and loving parent? Maybe so, but I was left wondering how close our relationship would prove to be. Will affection and love be enough to keep our attachment strong and relevant as she grows into adulthood? Sharing time is easy, but will I share important things about myself? Will she come to know me as a person and not just a parent; will she understand what matters to me as a human being? I have never found it hard to listen to my children, but perhaps I have fallen short when it comes to talking to them about myself. I do not expect or want them to become my confidants; I also have no doubt that a full and complete account of my psyche would propel them to new heights of boredom. But perhaps the man in the next booth had unwittingly given me the opportunity to recognize that my relationships with my children need to be fuller if they are to remain close.

As we drove back to the arena, Alexandra commented, "I'm glad we lost the bus, Daddy." I agreed and silently promised that she would never look back and remember me as a loving parent who became a stranger.

Recently, a report of a nontraditional career day for teenagers appeared in one of our national newspapers. In addition to women in fields such as engineering and the skilled trades, the list of participators included men who worked in traditionally female occupations, including a full-time male homemaker. My only complaint was that this workshop was entitled "Mr. Mom," unintentionally implying that fathers who take on domestic roles are crossing over into foreign territory. My hope is that we will soon reach the point where men who participate equally in family life are no more inclined to refer to themselves as "Mr. Mom" than women in the workforce refer to themselves as "Mrs. Dad."

Renegotiating Roles

Renegotiating roles in the home can be a very powerful way to reduce the stress and marital problems that arise when work and home are in conflict. The sooner this conflict is recognized as a joint problem the better; it is an invaluable early warning sign when it comes to averting chronic resentment and dissatisfaction.

While there has been a growing interest in the renegotiation of roles to reduce work-family conflict, it has nonetheless been tough going. Kenneth Dempsey at La Trobe University in Australia found women to be very receptive to asking their spouses to share in the housework. Men were not quite as receptive. In one study, only 4 out of 128 wives had any luck in their attempts to achieve a more equitable division of housework. Although men were resistant when confronted with such suggestions, another study noted that a sizable minority were more than willing to ask their wives to increase *their* workload even when their wives were already doing far more than their fair share. Such audacity was probably motivated by the expectation of success; although their wives viewed the requests as unreasonable, most eventually complied.

Dempsey could never be accused of not trying. The statistics were more favorable in a later study, which revealed that the number of men who increased their involvement in domestic tasks had risen to 40 percent. Typically, however, they would not assume full responsibility for the task, being content to be the "helper." This is a classic strategy that has nothing to do with a genuine lack of ability to handle the work on one's own; rather, it is the adult version of the duplicitous, thinly veiled, passive rebellion that children utilize instinctively when given a chore. The strategy is to pretend that the task is beyond the reach of your mental capacity and physical skills to ensure the other person quickly decides it would be easier to do it herself than enlist your help again.

The women discussed in Dempsey's research needed to take a crash course on renegotiation from their compatriots in a group studied by Betsy Wearing at the University of South Wales. These women were not interested in negotiation; change was achieved through "refusing to adopt a victim mentality by organizing and planning for self-space." This is the scholarly way of describing serious job action; the women went on partial strike when it came to housework and insisted that their spouses take on more of the child care.

Conducting workshops on stress management has given me the opportunity to talk to many women who feel that a revision of job descriptions is long overdue. Their thoughts, together with ideas from the research literature, led to my broadening the workshops to include an approach participants might use to renegotiate roles in their families. While it has been tried, it has not been formally tested. I do not guarantee results but hope it will provide at least some useful material. There are five core components:

The Attitude Adjustment

This warm-up exercise sets the tone. There are ten points to bear in mind:

- Taking on the Superwoman role is potentially damaging to the family because of the risk of chronic stress, depression, and burnout. Redistribution of responsibilities is a much better strategy.
- Gender boundaries reflect *choices*, not true differences between men and women.
- Women have cornered the market on guilt. Marriage requires the willingness to share; give some of it to your partner.
- Assumptions about innate differences between women and men are often wrong. The idea that women are less capable of competing in the workforce is as valid as the assumption that men cannot meet the emotional needs of their children.
- As a rule, employed women can expect to enjoy better mental and physical health than those who stay at home. Keeping yourself on the path to burnout, however, will prove that every rule has an exception.
- It really is true that men who participate fully in housework tend to be better adjusted psychologically. Look for *Vacuuming as Therapy* in the self-help section of your local bookstore.

- There is no evidence to support the view that men lack the gene needed to change diapers or clean toilets.
- The issue of who does the grocery shopping or the cleaning is *not* trivial. The feeling that the distribution of housework is unfair is a major source of marital conflict; no one likes to feel resentment every time they head off to the supermarket or plug in the vacuum cleaner. If it becomes chronic, marital conflict undermines the stability and well-being of the whole family.
- Fathers are not being asked to be "nice guys" or trendy "new age men" when roles are being renegotiated; they are being invited to take full advantage of the benefits and rewards of being closer to their children.
- A just and equitable family life is a right, not a request. Negotiation is the preferred way of effecting change, but strikes, work-to-rules, and rebellion are OK, too.

The Communal Approach

This is not the same as an equal division of housework and child care. The communal approach takes into account the total amount of time each person is working, no matter where this work is taking place. There has been justifiable criticism of some of the widely quoted statistics purporting to show that men are in a state of early retirement while women work a double shift. The fact that there has been inequity is not disputed; what has been criticized, however, is the selective use of data. For example, one study did not include the amount of time spent driving children to activities, which is commonly a task taken on by men. Other studies of dual-earner families have failed to consider the amount of time devoted to employment. When a difference between the parents exists, it is usually the man who spends more hours at his job and, therefore, has less time available for domestic work.

The goal of the communal approach is simple—resources, including time, are pooled. There can be assignments and schedules, but these are only guidelines. If the father puts the children to bed while his wife cleans up the kitchen, it does not follow that the first one to finish takes a break—everyone keeps going until all the work is done. Exceptions to this rule should, however, be allowed. While communal living is all about "pitching in," there will also be occasions on which one parent needs time away from the children and housework. The parent whose partner works very long hours away from home and is seldom there to take on domestic responsibilities is more than entitled to this consideration. Such situations may also require a discussion of priorities. The nature of a parent's employment may limit the options—some careers demand lengthy work weeks and prolonged absences from the home. In order to avoid resentment, however, it is critical that both parents feel that major decisions about home and work have been made jointly and that efforts will be made to share domestic tasks as often as possible.

Skill-Building

Let's face it, there is nothing that complicated about most aspects of domestic work, and the strategy of feigned incompetence to avoid taking on new responsibilities has already been discussed. At the same time, however, there can be situations in which a lack of opportunity or experience needs to be taken into consideration. Take cooking, for example. This is alien territory for a number of men and is usually not a hot topic when they get together. Chances are slim that a conversation between the guys in the locker room will begin with, "Hey, Chuck, I've got this wicked recipe for carrot muffins!" Men's experiences with cooking are likely to be limited to their insistence on taking charge of the barbeque. I personally believe this goes back to prehistoric times when the male hunter roasted mastodon ribs over the fire pit. The typical conversation of the avid barbequer is also quite unique—"let's fire up the old barbie" has a distinctly male ring.

On the other hand, traditionally male tasks can also be learned by women. The mysteries of the multi-headed screwdriver are fathomable for both genders, as are the intricacies of washing and waxing the family vehicle. It's a question of being willing to learn from one another and recognizing the benefits of versatility. The spirit of the communal model is that whoever is more available at the time does the work. Limiting skills so that only one person is the candidate for the job fosters inequity; it is also very impractical when both parents are employed and creates a modern-day twist to the "wait till your father (or mother) gets home" line.

A Partnership of Equals

The notion of "gate-keeping" has appeared in the discussion of obstacles to a fair division of domestic labor. The term refers to the possibility that, as much as women may want to work less, they do not want to allow their husbands to take over their territory. The resistance can stem from the belief that the job won't get done properly because of incompetence or indifference. The assumption of incompetence is embedded in our culture. Images of men struggling to change diapers have been used in many comedy shows, and one movie even depicted a three-man team failing at the task. A crying child will evoke the "she needs her mother" response from concerned onlookers; I have yet to hear "she needs her father." Yet skill-building, together with some discussion to establish mutually acceptable standards and procedures, should take care of this obstacle.

There is a danger that the notion of "gate-keeping" will be used as an excuse—this is the "I'd love to clean the toilets, but my wife won't let me" strategy. The only chance of getting away with this is if your spouse is unaware of the research indicating that gate-keeping is a minor obstacle compared to your resistance to taking on more tasks. It is nonetheless important for both parties to adopt the view that there is no "junior parent" or "assistant housekeeper." The assumption of competence encourages people to cross traditional gender boundaries. Entering the world of parenting may be as alien to some men as joining the ranks of engineering once was to women, but the more each gender encourages the other to enter foreign territory and assumes the ability to do so, the easier such excursions become.

Negotiation

Sometimes people seem to confuse negotiation with tirades. The essential difference is that the latter is an attack that highlights what other people are doing wrong, while the former consists of a reasonable request for what you want. Tirades are usually fueled by the mounting resentment arising from the feeling that one's partner is not doing his fair share of the work. They are often triggered by relatively minor events, such as a dirty dish left in the family room or forgetting to take the casserole out of the freezer. The problem occurs when these minor events become commonplace. The content of the tirade is predictable. With ample justification, it highlights the injustice of the situation and includes at least one sentence that starts with "I'm sick and tired of…" or "I've had it up to here with…" Tirades often have a volcanic momentum; once they get going, watch out! As mom erupts, dad and the children look on in astonishment and disbelief, unable to understand why the sight of a single used coffee cup has sent her over the edge. The climax is mom's announcement that she is going on strike and that everyone will have to fend for themselves. At this point, she storms off to the bedroom while dad reaches for the phone to order a pizza, at the same time reassuring the children that everything will be alright—he is sure that mom's condition is treatable. Mom's susceptibility to guilt almost guarantees that the strike will not be lengthy. Family life quickly resumes as normal—nothing changes.

Negotiation, on the other hand, emphasizes the presentation of one's position in a well-reasoned and solution-focused way. Studies indicate that both genders are more than capable of adopting this approach. This is women's preferred *modus operandi* at work, and they use it very effectively; the more emotional approach is reserved for home, and while it provides a legitimate way of venting, it often fails to bring about any solution.

The starting point for negotiation is to identify the problems to be solved—feeling resentful and stressed-out are more than sufficient. The second step is a combination of suggesting and asking for solutions. Given each person's hours of employment, how should domestic labor be divided and scheduled? As discussed earlier, assigning and scheduling are not meant to be rigid; they are, however, a means of avoiding a situation in which parents are either treading on each other's toes or completely neglecting a high-priority task.

Negotiation does not have to relate only to existing tasks and activities. Assume you have decided that you need set periods during the week when you can exercise or pursue a particular hobby or interest. Having explained your position, the next step in negotiation is simply to ask for what you want. In this case, the request is that your partner be with the children while you are out doing your thing. Most spouses would probably agree that this is a reasonable request. If yours is an exception, I refer you back to Betsy Wearing's study on page 44 and the head-on approach to securing more "self-space."

Some negotiations are more challenging than others. Housework, for example, can be a tough issue. Men have been much quicker to enter the realm of child care; the rewards are more obvious and direct. Housework is a different matter; as someone once quipped, "after making up beds two days in a row, the thrill is gone." Movement towards equity in this area of domestic life is likely to require assertion of the principles of justice and fair play, mixed with threats of serious job action.

A Matter of Choice

I am a strong advocate for fathers becoming more involved in family life; I believe that men can miss out on so much if they pass up the opportunity to share center stage in their children's lives. I also find the arguments for an equitable division of housework convincing on all fronts; apart from being fair, it makes for a happier life when the demands of work and home have become excessive. But I have not been appointed to speak for the parents of the world. Those who decide to differentiate roles on the basis of gender lines can obviously raise healthy, well-adjusted children, and I hope we never reach the point where our respect for those who prefer a more traditional model of family life is lessened. The critical variable is the agreement between spouses. Removing gender boundaries can be an important aspect of resolving the conflict between work and home, but it should not become the type of general and rigid rule it is intended to replace.

3 | Who's Minding the Children?: The Day Care Debate

Work-home conflict is a complicated thing. In addition to juggling multiple roles and combating persistent gender stereotypes, today's working parents must also cope with the day care debate.

Care or Abandonment?

Employed women may enjoy higher levels of physical and mental health, but these benefits can come at a cost. One of the obvious consequences of recent labor force trends was that someone else had to be found to look after the children while their mothers were at work. Stay-at-home fathers have always been a rarity, and chances are good that the majority of the preschoolers in your community spend part of their day being cared for by someone other than a parent.

Part of the challenge is finding care that meets the needs of the child while also accommodating the parents' work schedule. The most common problems are a shortage of affordable, high-quality day care and the challenge of finding last-minute care—for example, when a school-age child becomes sick. A significant number of women also report that the need for day care creates conflict when opportunities to advance their careers arise. Promotion can require more traveling, relocation, overtime, or extra responsibilities, all of which jeopardize the already tenuous balance between work and home.

Conflict relating to day care, however, is not about availability. A more important factor for many mothers is the belief that their entry into the workforce is potentially detrimental to their children, particularly during infancy. In spite of this concern, the trend is for mothers to return to work sooner after childbirth than ever before. More than 50 percent of infants and toddlers now spend in excess of twenty hours a week in the care of someone other than a parent; the number rises to almost 80 percent in the age three to six range. A mother's decision to return to her job in spite of the nagging concern that this decision is not in her child's best interests inevitably adds to her dilemma.

Also inevitable is the readiness of some experts and commentators to reinforce the mother's worst fears. Many are convinced that a link exists between the prevalence of day care and many of society's ills, including antisocial and aggressive behavior. They refer to the "downgrading of motherhood" and write doom-and-gloom articles about the new generation of unattached, lost children who are being abandoned by the legions of mothers who are flocking into the workforce.

In 1997, Penelope Leach's study of experts' views and assumptions regarding early child care appeared in the journal *Early Development and Parenting*. She contacted over four hundred members of an international organization of infant mental health professionals to survey their opinions regarding the best type of care for children in the first three years of life. The professionals were asked to assume that all types of care, such as staying at home with a parent or attending day care, were equally available and feasible. There was no doubt about the results—the experts were sold on lengthy at-home care by the mother and viewed any form of purchased care as less desirable. Fathers did not rate at all; they rarely made the shortlist of potential caregivers.

Preconceived notions like this make it difficult to obtain objective information about day care's true impact. Also contributing to the problem is the selective way in which data can be interpreted. A 1997 article in the *Washington Post* reminded me of Mark Twain's comment that there are "lies, damn lies, and statistics." Author Sherri Eisenberg highlighted how parents who embark on a search to find the truth about day care are likely to find themselves more confused than enlightened. She reviewed conflicting articles she had encountered. "Day Care Study Offers Reassurance to Working Parents" was probably welcome news in many households. Any feelings of relief would have been dispelled, however, on catching the headline "Day Care Study Offers 'Cautionary Note' to Mothers" or reading the line "None of the study's findings suggested that the children thrive in day care." As conflicting as they sound, these articles were based on the same study; the writers had been highly selective, both in the data they included and the way in which the results were portrayed. The reader thus received a very narrow and incomplete interpretation of what was in fact a complex study conducted by the National Institute of Child Health and Human Development. For understandable reasons, Eisenberg entitled her own article, "When It Comes to Day Care, You Can't Trust the Media."

Conflicting views about day care can be found in academic as well as popular writings. Claire Etaugh at Bradley University in Illinois reviewed more than one hundred psychology textbooks published since 1970. She found that the likelihood that sending children to day care would be depicted in an unfavorable light decreased over this time period. She undertook a similar review of prominent women's magazines over the past five decades. Early articles gradually became more supportive of mothers placing their children in day care. In the 1980s, however, the opinions expressed were often ambivalent, if not negative. This shift occurred around the time when day care was becoming the norm. By the mid-eighties, almost 50 percent of children under the age of one were receiving some form of day care for a portion of their week. In the same period, approximately 75 percent of the general public surveyed thought this was not a good idea; they believed the children should be home with their mothers unless extreme circumstances such as poverty dictated otherwise.

The fact that negative and ambivalent opinions about day care have been freely expressed is of considerable significance given the number of families utilizing it; the possibility that day care might damage children should not be automatically dismissed. If it is inaccurate, however, the negative image portrayed by those claiming to have knowledge in the area is yet another illustration of how so-called experts have created unnecessary guilt and added to the conflict between work and home.

The "Experts"—Separating Fact from Fiction

Before discussing what we actually know about the effects of day care, I want to defend my less than complimentary portrayal of experts. Although the directive "first do no harm" comes from the medical profession, I believe it should be adopted by all those in the child care field who are attempting to offer advice to parents. The term "expert" implies a degree of knowledge that may not exist. Within my lifetime, experts have convinced mothers not to breast-feed and have dismissed children's complaints of sexual abuse as fantasy. They have attributed autism and schizophrenia to poor mothering and have left many parents with a mountain of guilt as a result. Experts have stated with authority that girls are less intelligent than boys and have claimed that young women are physically unsuited to higher education or employment outside the home. Asked for their opinion on the matter, I am sure some would blame parents for the hole in the ozone layer and the near extinction of the Colorado squawfish.

I have to be careful not to sound overly critical. As a practicing psychologist with a large family and even larger debts, I cannot afford to be unemployed. I am also not cynical enough to believe that all child care advice is bad. I maintain that it is critical, however, for both parents and professionals to recognize how easy it is for intelligent, educated, and well-meaning people to give and follow advice that is irrelevant, misleading, or harmful.

It's also important to note that research never takes place in a vacuum. The early studies of the impact of day care often seemed to reflect the prevalent assumption that there had to be a problem. The role of the researcher was, therefore, to let us know how bad the problem was, presumably so that we could do something about it—perhaps by mounting a campaign to get mothers back at home where they belonged. But if you start with the assumption that the modern family is here to stay (at least for now), then it becomes far more productive to take a different perspective and ask how we can ensure that day care is a positive experience for both the children and the family as a whole. Fortunately, researchers have taken steps to answer this question, and their findings are a very valuable part of resolving the conflict between work and home.

The studies in this area span at least three decades and are extensive in both their number and scope. They include the U.S. National Longitudinal Survey of Youth that has been ongoing since 1979. This has involved more than 12,000 women and their families. In total, many thousands more have participated in the research, which has been conducted primarily in North America and Europe, and has encompassed aspects of children's development such as self-esteem, social adjustment, behavior at home and in the community, and school achievement.

All it takes is one course in psychology to make you realize that researchers rarely agree with one another. It's not that they are a crusty, argumentative bunch; it's just that the more you study an area, the more complicated it seems to get. The common experience that two studies yield different results is not necessarily a sign that one researcher got it right while the other messed up. An alternative, and highly plausible, reason is the presence of a factor that sent the results one way in the first study but in the opposite direction in the other. Social scientists like to call such factors "moderating variables," and recognizing their influence is essential to drawing conclusions about the effects of day care.

Infants and Toddlers

I would like to start with a discussion of the most controversial topic associated with the day care debate—attachment. You would be hard-pressed to find an introductory textbook in developmental psychology that does not refer to John Bowlby's classic work on early bonding and attachment. Beginning in the 1950s, his many publications revealed the importance of the infant's forming a strong, stable attachment. Given the extent of the gender boundaries that existed at that time, his work addressed the attachment between the infant and the mother. In keeping with the normal evolution of theory and knowledge, some of Bowlby's ideas have been challenged, and modifications have been suggested. Nonetheless, the importance of early attachment is now widely accepted. Forming this attachment is a process—not a one-shot deal like the imprinting of chicks to the mother duck. The day-to-day experiences with a loving, nurturing caregiver form the basis of a relationship that emerges as the child's primary attachment over the first year of life. From this perspective, placing a very young child in day care could be detrimental. But is this fear justified?

Before researchers could attempt to answer this question, they had to develop a way of measuring attachment. Psychologist Mary Ainsworth devised a method that has become the most widely used in the field. It is commonly referred to as the "Strange Situation." First of all, you have to upset the infant. You invite him over to play, mother in tow. Having transformed the room into a virtual toy store, you can be sure he will be having a ball. Now, instead of leaving well enough alone, you arrange for a stranger to enter the room, acting as if she should be allowed to join in the fun. In the meantime, mom slips out for a quick coffee. Chances are the infant will not be too impressed with these goings-on and will let his disapproval be known. Wondering why she ever consented to the study, mom comes back in while observers rate how readily the infant seeks her out and is comforted by her. If that were not enough, the whole process of separation and reunion is then repeated.

Children's reactions in the Strange Situation have formed the basis for categorizing the relationship between young children and their mothers. An attachment is seen as secure if the brief separation prompts the child to specifically seek out his mother on her return and if he is readily comforted by her. Varieties of insecure attachment have also been defined. The child may seem indifferent to his mother's presence or not take any comfort in her return.

The Strange Situation has been used in many studies conducted with children who have entered day care within the first few months of life when there has not yet been sufficient time to form a strong attachment to a parent. Some studies have indicated that the infants proceed to form just as secure an attachment as found among those remaining at home. Others, however, have reported insecure attachment. This is most likely to occur when mothers are working long hours, and boys may be at slightly higher risk than girls. But how strong is this effect? Alison Clarke-Stewart at the University of California reviewed the research, and her findings illustrate the need to distinguish between statistical and practical significance. On average, 36 percent of infants show signs of an insecure attachment when their mothers have full-time employment. The percentage drops for either part-time or stay-at-home mothers, but not below 29 percent.

There are other points to consider. How valid are the measures of attachment in the first place? This question has yet to be answered adequately, but it is notoriously difficult to find anything measurable in infancy that predicts something meaningful in the future. No one would suggest, for example, that the 36 and 29 percent of the infants in these studies all grow up to be alienated and insecure.

People in the field have also questioned the interpretation of the children's behavior in the Strange Situation. Perhaps day care teaches infants a certain resilience; they become used to regular, temporary separations from mom, become more accustomed to strangers in their environment, and are not so dependent on one person for comfort. All this could occur without any negative implications for the child-parent relationship.

More data will emerge. In the meantime, it seems safe to adopt the position that fits so often in this field—day care itself is not a problem. If there is a risk of weaker attachment, it probably relates to how stressed and exhausted a mother may feel if she has a full-time job on top of her family responsibilities. Feeling drained and depleted can affect the quality of the time that is spent together. If this analysis proves to be correct, implanting the fear that the attachment process will be damaged if an infant is in day care should be replaced with a gentler piece of advice—if you have full-time employment, do your best to organize your work schedule and home life so that you and your infant can have regular opportunities to relax, play, and otherwise enjoy each other's company. Provided these aspects of the relationship are not diminished, there seems little to worry about when it comes to utilizing day care services.

I have focused on attachment because of its significance for early development. Studies have also examined the relationship between day care and measures of cognitive and social growth. Some have reported lower scores among children in day care; others have not. A Swedish study, for example, found no relationship between day care and measures of personality and social adjustment among toddlers. The role of day care has also been studied extensively in the field of early intervention where the goal is to provide help to disadvantaged children during the preschool years. The beneficial effects that have been found are not only short term but also reduce the risk of later academic, social, and behavioral problems.

Research with children who come from more privileged families has also yielded positive findings. Clarke-Stewart reported that the social and intellectual development of very young children in day care centers was more advanced than that of children being cared for at home. (If your child is being cared for at home, do not panic and reach for the phone to sign her up for day care. She'll be fine. By the time she's settled into school, she should catch up; with the exception of children who come from disadvantaged families, day care, at best, gives the child a temporary edge.)

School-Age Children

The issues are different when it comes to school-age children. Now the age of the child emerges as one of the important factors. A valid summary statement would be that day care is not, of itself, an obstacle to the development and well-being of school-age children. In fact, it can exert a positive influence in this area. The majority of studies involving children aged three or four find that their subjects are as well, or even better, adjusted than peers who are not participating in day care.

Gender can sometimes complicate the results. Girls seem to thrive in day care, obtaining scores on tests of cognitive ability that equal or exceed those of girls being cared for at home. Although not a consistent finding, boys can show signs of lagging behind in this area of development; lower scores on measures of social adjustment have also been occasionally reported. But if you add another one of those moderating variables into the mix, it emerges that these negative effects can be overridden by the family. Parents often adjust their behavior in a way that averts potential problems. Once employed, they will organize their lives in a way that ensures there is no reduction in the time spent sharing activities with their children. When this is the case, cognitive and social development are not threatened.

The impact of day care on school achievement has been investigated in a number of studies. Typically, no differences are found. However, some researchers have noted that boys in day care seem to achieve at a slightly lower level than same-gender peers who are always in their parents' care. Whether or not this will be the case, however, has nothing to do with day care itself. You may be guessing the family is implicated yet again, and it is. The negative effect on achievement is not found when the influence of parental monitoring is taken into account. Boys who attend day care but also have parents who keep a close eye on their school work do not seem to suffer. The role of parenting style is once again highlighted, and the key elements of monitoring extend beyond keeping track of progress at school. They include having a more general awareness of the child's interests, knowledge of the child's activities and friends, and creating an atmosphere of open communication. The research also provides a simple but important piece of advice—because of their multiple commitments, some employed parents may not monitor their children as diligently as might otherwise be the case. Recognizing this, and making sure that the situation is rectified, should avoid potential problems.

Temperament, Change, and Prediction

Temperament—at least at its extremes—appears to be one of the few measurable characteristics of infants that may have long-term significance. There are, for example, enduring differences in how emotionally reactive infants are; they will also vary in other areas such as activity level, adaptability, attention span, and moodiness. A certain winning combination of traits gives you an "easy" child; this is the model child you show off to family and friends in the hope they have not read the research suggesting a genetic basis for temperament and will attribute her delightful manner to your exemplary parenting. If your luck is out, you have the challenge of a "difficult" child. This time, you hope that people *have* read the research and will blame her behavior on your spouse's gene pool. Yet another combination gives you the "slow-to-warm-up" model, while approximately one-third are so mixed up that they defy description.

There has been some interest in the relationship between temperament and how easily children will adjust to day care. The research is not extensive, but having an easy disposition may be an asset. Do not be surprised, however, if the relationship proves to be more complex. There is some suggestion, for example, that being "difficult" may not be such a bad thing. A child with this disposition may be particularly adept at drawing attention to himself and getting his needs met—at day care or at home.

Latchkey Kids

The latchkey or "self-care" child is not a recent phenomenon. The term has apparently existed for over two centuries and was coined to refer to children who actually had to lift a latch in order to enter their empty homes.

The number of children under thirteen who take care of themselves before or after school has risen steadily over the past three to four decades and is probably close to 10 percent. Some are very young; latchkey kids include children from kindergarten to adolescence. Once children reach the teens, however, they are usually not referred to as latchkey kids. The reason is that we often allow children to babysit at that age; we assume they are old enough to take care of themselves and others for at least several hours at a time.

This topic provides yet another example of how people in the same field can hold widely divergent opinions. One psychology textbook painted a disturbing picture of a terrified young child calling a hot line while hiding under his bed. Others, however, have argued that latchkey children have the opportunity to become more responsible and independent.

The results of the research are mixed; much depends on the individual child and the family and community in which he lives. A Canadian study of suburban children in the 1990s is typical of the research examining the relevance of community. Researchers Nancy Galambos and Jennifer Maggs at the University of Victoria compared sixth-grade children in self-care situations with those who were cared for by an adult. They studied the two groups during both the school year and the summer vacation months. Several measures of behavior, self-esteem, and social activity were included. The overall conclusion was that the two groups were very similar; the latchkey children did not appear to be suffering as a consequence of having to take care of themselves. Similar results have emerged from other studies of suburban and rural communities that also included children in younger grades. Most find no difference between self-care and adult care on measures of academic achievement, self-esteem, personality, behavior, and social adjustment.

Children in urban communities, however, can be more vulnerable. This is especially likely in neighborhoods with high crime rates and low community cohesion. Latchkey children in such environments are at greater risk for problems, including substance abuse.

Caution must be exercised, however. These results indicate trends; they do not necessarily apply to each child. There will be inner city children in tough neighborhoods who do not run into difficulty; there will also be children in the suburbs and rural areas who do not handle the responsibility of caring for themselves well. The research nonetheless points to the importance of considering the potential influence of the child's broader environment.

While finding no overall difference between the self-care and adult-care groups, Galambos and Maggs noted that the nature of the children's after-school activities was important. Both genders did just fine when they went straight home after school. I doubt that these children were reading mind-improving books or honing their housekeeping skills, but while they may not have put their time to good use, they weren't getting into trouble. Children taking the long way home so they could hang out with others who were also on the loose were more likely to prove that they had not used their time wisely. Girls, in particular, displayed more behavior problems and were prone to associating with a negative peer group.

This study illustrates yet another factor that has to be taken into consideration. The tendency for girls to stray from the straight and narrow was dependent on the family environment; it was not found among those exposed to the authoritative or "democratic" style of parenting. This style, which will be discussed more fully in Chapter 6, is characterized by parental warmth and acceptance combined with clear guidelines and assertive discipline. Children raised by democratic parents tend to be more confident in their ideas and opinions. They display greater self-reliance and possess better decision-making skills. Presumably these characteristics help them resist the negative pressures associated with being out in the community unsupervised.

How do you decide if you should allow your daughter or son to join the ranks of the latchkey kids? For some families, the decision may be forced by the lack of affordable alternatives. When there is greater choice, a number of questions can help reach an answer:

The Latchkey Checklist

- What is your child's age and maturity level? It would be hard to suggest an age below which self-care is never feasible—older does not necessarily mean wiser. Your child's track record with respect to being responsible and trustworthy at home and in other situations is a valuable source of data.
- How long will your child be unsupervised?
- What is your neighborhood like? Are you concerned about the type of people hanging out on the streets, or is yours a relatively safe community? Is the population largely transient, or do you have the benefit of a reasonably close-knit community in which people typically look out for one another?
- Do you feel confident that you can supervise your child at a distance? Does he have a clear understanding of what is unacceptable behavior, and has he learned from experience that there will be fair but definite consequences if he displays any of it? Are you able to contact him by telephone to provide an additional element of supervision?
- Can you establish routines and activities that meet your child's needs? Does she need a list of suggested activities to keep herself occupied? Can she have a friend over?
- Do you have a safety plan that he could recite chapter and verse? If he is able to prepare his own snack, can he use the stove or cutting knives safely? Should he answer the telephone? If so, what should he say if someone asks to speak to his mother or father? Does he understand the basic elements of street-proofing? Does he know the numbers to call in an emergency? Have you practiced the family fire drill recently? What neighbors can he contact if a problem arises? Can he be in all areas of the home? Is he allowed to play in the front or backyard? Can he visit a friend or ride his bike? How accessible can you

make yourself at work, and should he always call you when he arrives home? If necessary and affordable, would a pager or cell phone be advisable so that he can reach you at any time?

After you have considered all the important factors, you are left with one of those "judgment calls" that inevitably make parents anxious, at least until experience tells them they were right. Although the image of the child hiding under the bed is not representative of the latchkey kid, there are always risks involved when we allow our children greater freedom and independence. The research at least helps parents decide if self-care is an option.

Quality Control—What Is "Good" Day Care?

Perhaps the most important finding from the research surrounding day care is that separation from a parent is not, in itself, a problem. But it does not follow that day care will always be a positive experience. Poor quality day care—like poor quality care at home—is likely to be detrimental to children. Parents do not randomly select a center from the Yellow Pages or call the first number they find pinned up on a community bulletin board. The choices may sometimes be limited, but the process of selection reflects the wish to find the best quality of care available.

Parents are, in fact, quite selective if they are lucky enough to have a number of choices available. Those who opt for family day care tend to place the greatest emphasis on compatibility of child-rearing philosophy; this factor is easier to assess when only one person—typically a mother who is rasing her own children—will have part-time responsibility for raising yours. Another criterion high on the list is the presence of a home-like atmosphere. Preference for a center, on the other hand, often relates to the parents' emphasis on finding an enriching and stimulating environment. As I was reviewing this research, I was reminded of a friend who recently attended an open house for a nursery school program. He commented that the word "cognitive" seemed to find its way into every other sentence and that the theme of early stimulation and enrichment was prevalent in much of the presentation, as well as in the questions posed by prospective parents. I should add that both child-rearing philosophy and intellectual stimulation are likely to be important for all parents—it's just a question of how much weight is given to each.

A recent article in *Today's Parent* mounted an effective and much-needed defense for family day care providers. Author John Hoffman cited other articles in which readers had been warned about the threat of "every Tom, Dick, and Harry" opening a day care. As he pointed out, it sometimes seems as if family day care conjures up the image of a hoard of little ones scrambling to get a seat in front of the television while their chain-smoking custodian pours her next drink. His opinion that a family day care can be every bit as good as a program offered in a staff-run center is substantiated by a number of studies in North America and Europe. Typically, no differences are found on measures of the quality of interactions with the children or the level of verbal and cognitive stimulation.

One difference that does exist between the two types of care is the range in quality. Day care centers also vary in quality, but the range is narrower because of the extent to which they are regulated. The average quality of family day care, however, is not lower, and the woman next door may indeed be your best bet even if "cognitive" is not in her vocabulary.

Parents' criteria for evaluating quality will include many other factors, such as the training of the staff, the warmth and interest with which the adults relate to the children, and the physical environment, including equipment, safety standards, and nutrition. But what appears to be the most important determinant of parents' ultimate satisfaction is the extent to which they feel they have a good working relationship with the day care provider. Parents value exchange of information and ideas. They appreciate collaboration and want to feel that everyone is working together when establishing routines, implementing toilet training, or dealing with tantrums. The value placed on this relationship has led to a view of day care as a support for the family rather than a replacement.

But do any of these factors really matter when it comes to the impact of day care on a child's well-being and development? As always, finding a straight answer is a hopeless endeavor. In order to avoid a tedious account of the fine details of the inconsistencies, debates, and squabbles in the field, I would like to list the factors that are most likely to be related to whether or not day care will be a positive experience for a child:

The Day Care Quality Checklist

- Children-to-adult ratio: The commonsense view that, all else being equal, children will receive better care and attention when they do not have the adults hopelessly outnumbered is borne out in some, though not all, of the studies.
- Group size: Children seem to benefit when activities take place primarily in smaller groups. Being managed in herds is not quite so good, even if the ratio of children to adults is the same.
- Training and experience: This factor has to be considered carefully. Family day care can be just as effective as placement in centers. Although some family day care providers will have had formal training, most have not. Within day care centers, however, where many of the staff will not have had experience raising their own children, the level of training does appear to be relevant.
- Stability: Staff in day care centers tend to be poorly paid, and turnover can be a problem. Younger children, in particular, seem to benefit from the presence of adults they have come to know and can rely on to be there. One study with toddlers, for example, found that they were quite discriminating when it came to selecting whom they wanted to comfort them when they were upset or distressed. They tended to make a beeline for adults who had been there the longest and who had the lowest rates of absenteeism.
- Physical surroundings: A quick tour of a home or center is enough to determine if aspects of the physical surroundings—the general state of repair, the quality of the furniture, and the range of toys and other play materials—provide the type of environment you want for your child.

- Quality of interactions: It seems unnecessary to state that the way adults relate to the children in their care matters. Perhaps the key is the presence of an adult who sees herself as a lot more than someone who is running a storage facility for the temporarily orphaned. Children thrive on affection and stimulation.

The importance of being able to visit the day care as part of the selection process cannot be overstated. Sometimes parents are concerned that warm and attentive interactions are staged for their benefit; people do tend to be on their best behavior when they know they are being observed and evaluated. I take comfort from my belief that, while adults can role-play in this manner, young children will be themselves. Part of my practice involves assisting families and the court in making decisions about custody. Home studies are usually included in the assessments, and the difference between familiar and "staged" behavior is not hard to discern. The child who is accustomed to spending enjoyable time with a parent or day care provider will typically be enthusiastic and relaxed when they are sharing an activity; this is a normal, familiar part of their relationship. If, on the other hand, the caregiver would be hard-pressed to recall the last time she played with the children or read a story to them, expect to see signs of surprise or uncertainty on their faces. However nebulous and unscientific this may be, an environment in which people like and respect one another has a certain "feel" or "atmosphere," whether it is a home, day care setting, or classroom.

Gathering information about the factors that determine quality of day care has implications for setting standards for licensing and policies regarding staff training and programs. It can also help distinguish between what is necessary and what is desirable. For example, while parents might seek a program that has one adult to four children, a ratio this small has not been proven essential for ensuring that the day care facility can meet the needs of the children. While standards are needed, setting them unnecessarily high would add to the cost of day care and make them harder for many people to obtain.

Day Care and the Chicken Little Syndrome

The day care debate provides further confirmation of the spread of CLS. The accusation that mothers had abdicated their parenting responsibilities stemmed from the belief that deviating from the tried-and-true recipe threatened the welfare of our children. This assumption has proved to be incorrect, but it lingers. Those advocating a return to the days of the stay-at-home mom are smaller in number, but they still constitute a sizable and vocal minority. Over 40 percent of those surveyed recently by a Canadian national newspaper endorsed the statement, "Families would be in much better shape if mothers would only stay home with their children." The research, however, tells us that day care and callous abandonment of one's offspring are not one and the same thing; as wonderful as you may be as a parent, your child will not grow up to be any more dysfunctional than the rest of us if she is cared for by someone else when you work. Furthermore, employment typically does not have a negative impact on the amount and quality of the time parents spend with their children. In fact, employment can *add* to the quality of family life. It provides financial benefits for everyone; it also can be an important part of the mother's identity. Women who enjoy working typically benefit from resuming employment; their children also benefit from having a happier mom.

I also find it reassuring that employment does not negate the influence of the family; time and time again, the studies point to the significance of family life in determining the impact of day care or the implications of becoming a latchkey kid. Parents do make a difference, even when they are not physically present. There are many ways of raising healthy, well-adjusted children, and one of them is to form a partnership with a day care provider.

4 | Taking Care of Ourselves I: Time Management

The number-one complaint of most parents is that they simply do not have enough time for themselves. They want more opportunity to be with their families, and they find themselves neglecting friends and abandoning recreational activities in order to get it. Given that time is such a precious commodity, it makes sense to manage it as wisely as possible.

Mikal McLaughlin and her colleagues at Maryland's Frostburg University interviewed a group of employed mothers to determine the strategies they used to manage time. They found that women who were familiar with a number of time-management strategies—and used them regularly—experienced less stress and reported greater marital satisfaction. The latter finding might seem surprising; working on time-management skills is probably not high on the priority list for someone wanting to revitalize a marriage. As the authors point out, however, two-career couples have the highest rate of divorce; one factor seems to be the lack of closeness and support that results from their limited opportunities to be together. Furthermore, if one or both partners are experiencing stress because of the demands of their work and family responsibilities, it can eventually put strain on the marital relationship.

As for the strategies themselves, McLaughlin and her colleagues distinguished between eleven specific approaches to time management. These included making "to do" lists, budgeting time so that it is distributed according to the importance of each task, asking others for help, prioritizing tasks, re-prioritizing them as needed, and saying "no" to additional tasks and requests for your time.

Other studies have looked directly at the impact of effective time management on stress specifically resulting from work-home conflict. It seems that the level of stress is reduced the more people feel they are in control of their time. The critical factor is the sense of "mastery"; it does not have to follow that the person becomes more efficient, although this can be a bonus. The mere perception of being on top of things, rather than being overwhelmed by them, understandably makes for a much happier life.

This chapter represents an attempt to apply what we know about time-management strategies to family life. In a number of instances, the ideas have come from workshop participants; there is rarely a shortage of suggestions when people start brainstorming about ways to alleviate the stress in their lives.

Setting Priorities and Cutting Corners

Many of us need to hone our skills when it comes to cutting corners. First of all, you need to develop the right attitude and get rid of the nagging thought that this is a bad thing. Give it an honest try; it's one of the favorite exercises in workshops, and once people get into it, they are hooked.

The exercise begins with writing down everything you do during a typical work week. Cover each day fully, from the time you get up until you fall into bed exhausted. Then go through the list and underline which activities are *absolutely essential* for maintaining your lifestyle. Obvious examples would be getting the children to school, going to work, and doing the grocery shopping. Next, give a five-star rating to activities that, while not essential, are worthwhile and enjoyable enough to keep on the list. Common items in this category would be people's hobbies, recreational pursuits, and activities with the kids. Take a long hard look at what's left over and ask yourself the following questions:

- Would it be life-threatening to strike this activity off the list or at least do it less frequently?
- If I could be sure my mother would not find out, would I gladly omit this item?
- If my mother did find out, have I now reached the point in my emotional development where I could respond to her disapproval with a polite version of "Tell someone who cares"?

Over the years I have found that the most common "leftover" items relate to housekeeping. Take vacuuming for example. (If this falls into your "most cherished" category, I'm afraid I cannot help you—look for a top-notch therapist and join a support group.) I am the founding member and president of S.A.V.E.D.—Society for the Abolition of Vacuuming Every Day. This society was not founded on a whim but reflects solid research. Two findings are central to S.A.V.E.D.'s mission. The first is that it is impossible to have a truly clean house. I came to this conclusion after reading *The Secret Family* by David Bodanis. This book is not for the squeamish or faint of heart; it documents how one's home is far from being a castle. Did you know that we are surrounded by millions of little creatures that are permanent, uninvited guests? Consider the omnipresence of dust mites. They are invisible to the naked eye; this is fortunate because they are *very* ugly when seen through an electron microscope. The point I am getting to is that, no matter how hard you try, no matter how many times you vacuum, no matter how much you dust, and no matter how many expensive filtering systems you purchase, you cannot get rid of all the dust mites in your home. I even went so far as to purchase one of those vacuum cleaners that promises to take out 99.97 percent of what it sucks up. This may sound wonderful, but since the number of dust mites in your home exceeds the combined populations of China and India, that .03 percent remaining is a force to be reckoned with. This book made me realize that dirt and infestation are part and parcel of daily life and that the goal of keeping a clean house is, in reality, futile.

The second empirical underpinning of S.A.V.E.D. does not take as long to explain. It is simply this: in the exhaustive research I have conducted since last Tuesday, I can find no study showing a link between how many times parents vacuum each week and the adjustment of their offspring in either childhood or adulthood. It just does not matter.

While I am not advocating squalor, I have been struck by the number of workshop participants who have come to the realization that their daily housekeeping routines are unnecessary and burdensome. In the days when most homes had a full-time homemaker, such routines would have been much easier to accommodate, especially when the children reached school age. The same routines do not fit as readily into the schedules of working parents.

I chose to talk about vacuuming first because most people are open to eliminating this chore as far as possible. I will now be braver and tackle the "sacred cow" of modern family life—the family meal. I am not convinced by those experts who insist that the daily family meal is the hallmark of good parenting. As much as I love the image of love and warmth being passed around with each heaping bowl of home-cooked fare, how realistic is this for the average overworked parent?

Let it be known that I take my food very seriously. Of all the human passions, eating is the least complicated. The first bite of a chocolate eclair is as close to an out-of-body experience as I need get, and images of food sustain me through my darkest hours. Such visions, however, can be shattered by the reality of the family evening meal. It begins with a simple question as the children walk through the door: "What's for supper tonight?" This is no innocent request for information. It is a signal to slip into "auto-whine" as soon as the menu is disclosed. Yes, they love chicken at grandma's, the local fast food joint, and their friends' houses, but mine tastes different. Why do they even have to look at broccoli, let alone put something so disgusting into their mouths? And don't I realize that casseroles are an affront to human dignity and a violation of their rights? Protests duly ignored, we gather at the table. One of the unwritten rules is that we share not only the meal but also the experiences of the day. While I am certainly open to conversation, what would be so wrong with eating in silence? Whole orders of monks do it and their life expectancy is above the norm. I suspect that the children share my point of view. There are days when I swear they have no recollection of even going to school. If they remember doing anything, it is either "not much" or "the usual stuff." While Kathy and I treat such comments as communication break-throughs, they hardly constitute witty repartee or stimulating debate. Consider also what transpires when one of the children actually starts talking in sentences. Either the others all join in at once, competing furiously for air time, or the speaker embarks on a monolog that finally prompts us to issue the gag order, "Eat your food before it gets cold."

Let me assure you that I am not advocating the abolition of family meals. What I am suggesting is that there are times when priority should be given to reducing the stress often experienced by working parents when they rush home to start the second shift. There are alternative ways of ensuring that children are fed and watered on those occasions when there is little time to prepare a traditional meal. "Grazing" is one. While an accepted practice among beasts of the field, the potential benefits of grazing have been ignored in child care books. Grazing is particularly useful when confronted with a picky eater. We have a son who used to hold a record for the length of time during which a green vegetable had not passed his lips. Getting him to eat vegetables at mealtimes often developed into a set of complex negotiations. A compromise would eventually be reached—we would all go in peace once he had eaten half of his broccoli. But life is rarely that simple. Heated debates would ensue. Aaron's definition of "half" would rarely meet ours; the fact that his mother teaches math and should, therefore, have a good working knowledge of fractions failed to impress him.

Grazing became our salvation. Upon returning with the children from school, it was a simple matter to set a plate of raw vegetables (which can be prepared ahead of time) and dip conspicuously on the kitchen table. No direction to come and eat had to be given; the children were hungry and while vegetables might not be their first choice (no fast food chain ever built its name on serving vegetables and dip), they were the only nourishment available.

After taking time to catch our breath and relax for a few minutes, the next phase would be preparing a plate of fruit or cheese and crackers. For variety, yogurt, granola bars, muffins, or a bowl of applesauce might appear on the table. There would be no discussion of "mealtime" or any expectation that everyone sit down together to eat. At the end of the process, all major food groups would be more than adequately covered, the children would be content, and we would not feel that we had taken yet one more step on the road to burnout.

Grazing can be a hard sell if parents believe it will detract from the amount and quality of time they spend with their children. My counterargument would be that having a more relaxed introduction to the evening activities can be an excellent prelude to spending time with children in other ways, such as reading together, playing games, or even just sitting down and cuddling on the couch while watching a television show.

Grazing can also be a shared activity. I once had a client who grew up in a single-parent family. Here is his description of "family grazing."

My mother and father separated before I became old enough to remember ever living with two parents. Being raised by just my mother was, for me, normal—although society gradually taught me that I was not supposed to feel that way. Over the course of my childhood I came to detest the term "single parent." I became aware that single mothers were often viewed as somewhat inferior to their married counterparts who lived in "intact" families. What I would now label as stereotyping was then experienced as a vague feeling of being somehow inferior—a second-class citizen.

I doubt that my mother ever purchased any of those magazines and books that are supposed to set people on the path to perfect parenting and exemplary home-making. Her guiding principle was "unless it's life threatening, why get upset?" From this perspective, there was very little that actually had to be done and if my mother ever experienced so much as a twinge of guilt at her failure to orchestrate the traditional family meal after returning from a full day's work, she hid it well. In fairness to my mother, I am sure she did prepare regular meals at times, and I know we had a table and chairs in our eat-in kitchen. But my recollection of traditional mealtimes is overshadowed by the memory of our blanket suppers.

We all had chores in preparation for this event. My brother would get the large quilted blanket from my mother's bed. I would help mom with the menu; this meant grabbing a package of crackers, a jar of peanut butter, or that processed-beyond-recognition-devoid-of-all-essential-nutrients-spread-at-your-own-risk-cheese, a jug of milk, three glasses, knives, and plates. To ensure that the major food groups were covered, my mother might add mini-carrots (no cutting or other preparation required) and the fruit bowl. All chores completed in under four minutes, and with supper laid out on the coffee table in the family room, we would sink into the couch, one on each side of mom, and cover ourselves with the blanket.

Rules of etiquette were different, but they nonetheless existed. If you wanted to add flavor to a carrot, a dollop of cheese spread or even peanut butter was quite acceptable, but double-dipping was out. While you didn't have to ask for something to be passed to you, reaching over in a way that blocked someone's view of the television was frowned upon. And, thinking of the television, although conversation was permitted and welcomed, it was not required. My mother would appoint one of us to take the channel changer and find a "mindless" show to watch. I am assuming that after a long day at work the educational channel was not on her agenda, and she seemed more than content to have no greater intellectual challenge than Tom and Jerry *or* Gilligan's Island *reruns.*

> *My brother and I appear to be healthy adults. Neither has been diagnosed with scurvy or rickets, somehow we know how to behave reasonably well in restaurants, and each of us has received repeat dinner invitations. We have also survived other consequences of our mother's "if it ain't life-threatening" philosophy—such as the fact that she never wore out a vacuum cleaner or exposed herself to the risk of stress-related illnesses by allowing the sorry state of our bedrooms to become a test of her authority and control.*
>
> *I can still recall the time when I finally realized that the term "security blanket" was an abstract concept—a metaphor people used to express the need to feel comfortable and protected. Up until that moment, I had believed that it referred to an actual blanket, just like my mother's.*

Another alternative to the family meal is aimed at countering the extent to which couples seem to lose sight of the importance of spending time with one another. While we may have severed ties with the Brits, occasionally borrowing their traditional version of "supper time" has merit. We have friends who have already adopted this custom of eating after the children. Kate and John eat together regularly. Their children appear healthy, and I assume they are fed and watered before being sent off to occupy themselves. I'm told that John never whines about the menu, and that Kate even smiles if peas are put on her plate. They have perfected the art of synchronized eating and talking. John moans loudly as he takes his first bite of an eclair, and Kate understands. Kate and John are happy people.

Slowing Down the Hurried Child

For the past month, Tuesday evenings have required precision timing. Watches are synchronized, and a flat tire would throw everyone's life into complete disarray. Alexandra is whisked out of the gym as soon as her after-school basketball game or practice is over and driven directly to her piano lesson. During the course of the ten-minute car ride, she eats an early supper (the portable, grazing variety) and completes her creative writing assignment (her account of how often and how much she practiced the piano that week). I drop her off wondering why Kathy and I cling to the idea that, in spite of the battles that arise whenever we so much as suggest she venture into the living room to see if the piano is still there, music lessons will enrich her life. As I arrive home, Kathy is returning from work only to head out almost immediately with Kiera, who has to get to the first of her three dance classes. I collect Aaron, who is off to band. Provided all the lights are green, I retrieve Alexandra on time and listen to her complain that, no matter how many scales she eventually learns, her teacher always seems to come up with a new one. She changes into her dance clothes as we drive over to collect her friend and fellow car pool member. After dropping them off at their dance class, Kathy and I have time to come home and rest for a good ten minutes before the return trips, snacks, and homework routines have to be organized.

Tuesday evenings are not our favorites, and I am sure similar scenes are acted out regularly by many families. We live in a culture that emphasizes "quality time" and early opportunity. We also live in a society where children are supervised far more closely than before. From the age of six or seven, my brother and I were allowed—if not actively encouraged—to spend weekends out with friends, playing at the park, trekking through the local conservation area, or simply roaming. Our parents were not negligent or permissive, although they could easily be seen as such by modern standards. The term "streetproofing" had yet to find its way into the language, presumably because the world was not believed to be as menacing and threatening to young children as it is today.

The idea that we overorganize and "program" our children was the subject of a recent article in *Time*. In "The Quest for a Superkid," authors Jeffrey Kluger and Alice Park wrote of children filling what few spare hours they have with a "buffet line of outside activities that may or may not build character but definitely build résumés. Kids who once had childhoods now have curriculums." Kluger and Park relate this trend to the increase in the number of mothers who work and their guilt at feeling they are neglecting their children. Although I would not doubt this is a factor, the view that children are too programmed has a longer history. David Elkind began writing about the "hurried child" in the early 1980s and later published a book with the same title. He deplored the "increasing and unrelenting stress on today's young people" and was critical of parents for burdening their children with excessive and unrealistic expectations.

Much of what is written on this topic points an accusatory finger at parents. Whether the excessive programming stems from guilt or a relentless drive to create a Superkid, parents are held to blame. Although I am all for the idea that we should accept responsibility for our actions, I don't believe that enough attention has been paid to the role of those ever-present and much-too-vocal experts. More than five million copies of a book that promises to teach babies to read have been sold. The cover shows a mother holding a flashcard with the word "nose" in front of her daughter, who looks no more than six months old. The smiling child has her finger in close proximity to her nose, and the authors hope that the potential purchaser of the book will interpret this as an indication of literacy. Personally, I believe the baby is engrossed in the type of socially unacceptable body exploration that infants engage in with abandon. The authors stress the need to stimulate the reading pathways as soon as possible, but in spite of their claims to be pioneers in the field of child brain development, they present no objective data. The reader is cautioned not to start before the baby is three months old—after all, you don't want to rob her of her childhood. For variety, the baby's curriculum can be expanded. Her math should be coming along quite nicely by six months and, to make sure she does not become too specialized, the authors offer a sequel guaranteed to give encyclopedic knowledge.

Now that I'm on a roll, why wait until the child is born? There is nothing like a few words *in utero* to get the fetus off to a good start. If plants can thrive when exposed to Beatles music, just think what a few readings from *War and Peace* (with Mozart playing in the background, of course) could do for the embryonic brain. To ensure that your offspring is paying attention, you could also purchase a pregaphone. A cross between a megaphone and a stethoscope, this device is placed in the vicinity of the navel to open the channels of communication between parent and child.

Although I have picked extreme examples, the insistence that we are at risk for missing golden, once-in-their-lifetime opportunities to stimulate and enrich our children has added unnecessary pressure to family life. A middle ground is needed. Parents will always want to give their children opportunities to learn and explore, and they certainly do not want them to be left behind. I find some relief, however, in the lack of evidence supporting the idea that we can spur on a child's brain development through endless stimulation. It seems more likely that maturation is the key factor, which means you might as well wait until the time is right. This sentiment is not new; concern about the tendency to force too much learning on children led one nineteenth-century writer to warn about the dangers of attempting to "develop the flower before the stalk is grown."

The recommendation is not that children quit their karate and music lessons to sit around aimlessly waiting for the stalk to grow. A redefinition of "quality time" may, however, be in order. Kate Douglas Wiggin, the author of *Rebecca of Sunnybrook Farm*, wanted children to have the type of life depicted in her novels. Although her view that "a child has a right to a genuine, free, serene, healthy, bread-and-butter childhood" might sound overstated, it reminds me of the importance of taking a more relaxed approach to child-rearing. According to the "bread-and-butter test" the following items would qualify as quality time.

The Quality Time Checklist
Activities just for children:

- Talking on the telephone to a friend and taking half an hour to say absolutely nothing
- Eating popcorn while watching *101 Dalmatians* for the fifty-third time

- Lying on the bed, staring up at the ceiling, and rarely showing signs of intelligent life
- Calling the same friend back with renewed lack of purpose
- Going to the mall with a friend and seeing just how many bargains and treasures you can buy at the Dollar Store with your allowance
- Building a fort in the basement
- Hanging out with friends

Activities to share with your child:

- Playing "store" without expounding theories of microeconomics and business management
- Play fighting, tickling, and other tomfoolery
- Playing yet another round of Go Fish or some other game that requires no more than two functioning neurons
- Sleeping together in the fort and (as you may have guessed) not explaining the fundamentals of building construction and engineering
- Chit-chatting about nothing deep or memorable
- Walking in the park
- Sitting down together in the same room and seeing what happens
- Competing to see who can sleep in the latest on Sunday morning

Although Kathy and I will continue to sign our children up for activities, we have made unscheduled time equally as important. It can be illuminating to add up the total amount of time (and money) that has to be found to support programmed activities. An additional exercise is to determine how much time is spent shuttling back and forth; "I feel like a taxi service" is a common lament.

Reducing the amount of scheduled time can go a long way to reducing the work-family conflict. It also benefits children—they need to learn how to organize their own time and be part of making up the rules when they play with other children. Such experiences promote independence and cooperation, and are a crucial part of preparing children for school. Some educators even argue that these areas of development are more important than trying to teach children to read before they set foot in kindergarten.

Children also need opportunities to simply use their imaginations. At times, they need to be still or cuddle up with a parent for a lot longer than is possible when bedtime is squeezed into an already overbooked day. Hurried children and their hurried parents can lose sight of the fact that cutting back on scheduled time creates rather than misses opportunities.

The Recruitment Drive and Child Labor

Today, child labor may be seen as exploitation, but not that long ago many families simply could not afford to support their children. Sons and daughters either worked in the home or contributed the meager earnings they could obtain from outside employment. Even very young children were more likely to be employed than schooled. Today, a three-year-old who can remember to hang up her coat, take her dishes to the sink, and flush—all on the same day—is applauded. Two hundred years ago, the same child could have been employed as a bird-scarer or goose girl. Youngsters finding themselves in such positions functioned very much as adults; in many important respects, their roles could not be distinguished from those of their parents.

Historically, children have also been able to demonstrate skills far in advance of those required for scaring birds or rounding up geese. By the age of ten, they could be accomplished assistant farmers who were expected to miss school during critical times of the year such as sowing and harvesting. Others might be apprentice wheelwrights or blacksmiths, capable of tasks that required complex visual and motor skills.

I must be careful not to contradict myself. I do not think of such times as the "good old days," and we are not encouraging our eleven-year-old to drop out and pursue a career in chimney sweeping. But even Rebecca had the odd chore or two down on Sunnybrook Farm, and sometimes we forget that children are capable of learning many skills at a relatively young age. In modern-day households where there's too much work to go around, it is entirely reasonable to expect the children to pitch in.

At this point, I'd like to refer you back to the list of activities compiled during the cutting corners exercise. The list should have been culled, but it probably remains lengthy. A family meeting and recruitment drive are now in order. The goal is a just and equitable outcome. Unless there is an urgent need for a bird-scarer, a three-year-old's job description may be limited to assisting with tasks such as cleanup after supper, tidying his room, and feeding a pet. At the other end of the spectrum, the teenager with a driver's license can head off to the grocery store, transport younger siblings, and have a range of responsibilities that encompass the home and community.

I am not totally obsessed with food, but I would like to return to the topic of eating for a moment. We've already discussed how the rush to prepare meals is a common beginning to the "second shift." Younger children can assist, and once their apprenticeship is complete, they can take a turn preparing the family meal. Although I am not willing to admit it to his face, Aaron, at seventeen, has fine-tuned his skills to the point where his pasta sauce is better than mine. After many years of kitchen duty, it is such a pleasure to have a meal cooked for us. It also has reaffirmed our belief that there is justice in the world; however petty this may seem, we have been known to chuckle quietly when Aaron gets irate because the rest of us don't hurry to the table after he has called us for supper.

You should go into the recruitment drive with your eyes open. Be prepared for resistance. Do not expect to hear, "I'm so glad we had this meeting. Thank you for giving me the opportunity to contribute to the household and, in some small way, repay you for everything you do for me. I think I'll skip going out with my friends today and get right to my jobs." Resistance can take the form of feigned incompetence. Most of us are familiar with this strategy, although we would probably deny it under cross-examination. I have no interest in disproving Kathy's view that I am incapable of doing the laundry without shrinking the most expensive item of clothing in the pile; for her part, Kathy shows no sign of mounting a coup to oust me from my position as cook. So do not be surprised if your otherwise bright, resourceful, and self-confident child acts as if the intricacies of pushing a broom are beyond him. If children can play computer games without reading the instructions, navigate the Internet, and program a VCR, surely they can master the complexities of a washer and dryer or microwave oven?

Resistance can also take the form of "it's not fair." Older siblings can complain that they have more to do than younger ones. Assignment of tasks and expectations, however, should be based on age and development. This guiding principle is used outside the family as well; the student in grade three does not have as much homework as one in grade twelve. At home, he goes to bed earlier and does not get to use the car; but neither does he have to mow the lawn or do the laundry. When he gets older, he too will have the responsibilities and privileges that come with age—he can also expect to inherit the chores left behind when his sibling moves out.

Sometimes parents worry that they will be burdening their children by recruiting them into the family workforce, robbing them of what little is left of their childhood. Family therapists will talk about the dangers of creating a "parental child," often in relation to single-parent families. When I read about the higher levels of maturity, independence, and responsibility that have been found among adolescents in single-parent families, however, I am left wondering if those in two-parent households are pampered. One of the articles I read during my family therapy training discussed the value of involving older children in the running of a single-parent home when there are younger siblings. The author pointed out that, back in the days when large families were commonplace, it was normal for older siblings to share responsibility for the younger members of the family. The analogy of a political democracy was also used to refer to the establishment of a cabinet in which the single parent was the prime minister, while the older children were junior ministers. She was not naive in suggesting this title; no teenager is going to beam with pleasure at the prospect of ministerial status when all this entails is the right to wash the kitchen floor. But being in the cabinet also meant having a junior role in decision-making—perhaps being consulted about the day-to-day running of the house or being asked for an opinion when deciding how to spend extra money. The term "junior ministers" highlights the importance of guidance and supervision—reminding the parent that, in spite of their newfound independence, teenagers still need support, understanding, and direction. With this in mind, cabinet meetings are not solely about assigning duties or reaching decisions, they also create an opportunity for the parent to focus on the needs of her ministers.

In addition to fostering independence, involvement in running the house has a positive impact on children's social development. This effect has been noted by Joan Grusee and her associates at the University of Toronto. Adolescents who were assigned work that benefited the whole family were rated relatively high on a measure of the concern they had for other people. What may seem like a chore can, in effect, be one of those valuable learning experiences that children need—it really is for their own good, as well as reducing the stress on their working parents.

It can sound like a huge leap to connect division of the family workload to bonding and attachment, but let me give it a try. I have a preference for shared labor at home. There will, of course, be times when children have sole responsibility for a chore and will be expected to display independence. But there can also be opportunities to work together. Last weekend, Aaron and I worked together cleaning up the backyard. He played his music, and I kept my comments to myself. His silent suffering was interspersed with conversation, and his rate of finding excuses to take a break was far less than when he is out there on his own. The job was finished with a minimum of fuss, and he was good company to boot.

The term "togetherness" does not typically conjure up images of conjoint dishwashing, laundry folding, and bathroom cleaning, but I suggest at least entertaining this expanded definition. Being together does not have to apply only to recreational and other "fun" activities; many parents want more time with their children, and redistributing the workload can help accomplish this goal, while simultaneously reducing the demands on the overworked members of the family.

Gender Boundaries Revisited

One of the pressing issues in our family is whether or not Kiera, who is now fifteen, will be expected to operate the lawnmower and snowblower when she is the senior child-in-residence. Negotiations are starting early. Aaron is scheduled to leave when he completes high school next year. Whether or not he pursues his education, his passion for golf, or the woman of his dreams is immaterial—he is going. It's not that we don't love him dearly; it's just that we have passed a family bylaw that prohibits living with our adult children.

The lawnmower issue is being hotly debated. Kiera, who by no means has been brought up in a traditional family, shows no hesitation or compunction when asserting that operating such machines is a "boy's job." I am getting worried. If she prevails in instating stereotypical gender roles, I will have to face the fact that I am the only male left.

It is common for gender bias to be evident in assignment of household chores, even in families where the parents genuinely hold egalitarian attitudes. As might be predicted, cutting the grass, small repairs, and washing the car are often designated as "male" tasks and given to fathers and sons. "Female" tasks such as cleaning and cooking are more likely to be carried out by a mother or daughter.

Ignoring traditional gender boundaries during the recruitment drive has two advantages. The first is that no one can get away with using gender to claim that he is not qualified for the job. The second is that it helps create an atmosphere of gender equality, with all of its attendant benefits. Perhaps I should apply this line of reasoning with Kiera, although I doubt she will be convinced that each time she starts the lawnmower she will be striking a blow for feminism.

Lists, Schedules, and Just Saying "No"

Making to-do lists and ordering the items according to importance are simple skills that often crop up in time-management literature. I do not have much to add. The process is hardly complicated; if you want to get fancy, you can even allocate an amount of time to each item. The only thing I would add is a cautionary note. As much as lists can help you utilize your time more effectively, they can also make your life miserable. I never have to give myself a hard time about not completing all the items on my list because I never make one. For the more organized person, a list can also serve as a reminder of what has not been accomplished. It can contribute to a feeling of failure; putting the item on the list was a commitment not kept. Such ways of thinking probably account for the studies indicating that lists and schedules can add to parents' stress rather than alleviate it.

It's all a question of attitude. If you view the list as a carved-in-stone solemn oath, you could be in for trouble. You will feel compelled to complete all the items—on time no less—or admit defeat and failure. If the foregoing applies to you, vow never to make another list—unless you feel you do not have enough guilt and self-reproach in your life. If, on the other, you are the kind of person who is unlikely to be tyrannized by a list, give it a try.

There is one list I do advocate for more general use. The cutting corners exercise starts with eliminating items from a list, and the recruitment drive is the process of transferring some of the other items to someone else's list. But the end result will never be a blank piece of paper. I like to end workshops with asking people to imagine that the day had twenty-six rather than twenty-four hours. I ask them to decide how they would use this extra time. As part of making their list, I suggest they imagine being interviewed during their retirement years. The interviewer asks them to look back on their adult lives and talk about their greatest successes and biggest regrets.

The idea for this exercise came from Harry Chapin's song *Cat's in the Cradle*. Chapin's lyrics tell the story of a father who never seemed able to find enough time for his son. Other things got in the way. He was busy building a career, and there would always be another day to play ball. But somehow there wasn't. His son grew up and moved away. The last verse conveys the sadness the father feels when he realizes that it is too late—he now wants a closeness they will never have. His son, however, has his own life—a life in which his father will never have more than a minor part.

The fact that the most frequent complaint of both working mothers and fathers is that they do not have enough time for their families does not make it hard to predict the outcome of this exercise. Most participants would use the time to be with the people who matter the most to them; children seem to head the list, with spouses coming in a close second.

Knowing what your priorities are does not, of course, mean you can always make the necessary changes. Finding those two extra hours is not an easy task; neither is cutting corners nor slowing down. But heightening our awareness of our priorities can make it easier to stand our ground when it comes to saying no. There is, however, no simple or quick solution. The employee who wants to cut back his hours has every right to march into his boss' office and turn down a new assignment or announce that he is cutting back to part-time. However, the boss may also exercise her right to wish him well in his new job.

The choices aren't easy, but they have far-reaching implications. In *Values Shift: The New Work Ethic and What It Means for Business*, John Izzo writes about a modern-day paradox. Although people attach more importance than ever to having a fulfilling career, they also want to draw a protective line around their personal and family lives. He interprets the fact that the majority of young adults graduating from college state they would not allow work to become more important than family life as a sign of a growing determination to say no to excessive demands on our time.

Like many parents, I struggle to maintain a reasonable balance between all those areas of my life that demand my time. I am slowly getting there. I do not work the hours I used to. I decided several years ago to keep any form of individual community service to an absolute minimum; as far as possible, evenings and weekends will belong to my family for as long as they care. When I look back, my response to that "if you could do it over again..." question already includes a regret that I have often failed to draw that line around my personal life. On the positive side, there's nothing like regret, tinged with guilt, to make us open to instigating rather than postponing change. Time is such a limited, precious, and non-renewable commodity, and this isn't the dress rehearsal.

5 Taking Care of Ourselves II: Stress Management

I recall my first trip to the new health store in our local mall. The shelves were stocked with products designed to alleviate every conceivable human ill, including insomnia and anxiety, loss of libido, and irritability. Just walking around gave me a sense of hope, and by the time I brought my basket to the checkout I was actually imbued with a sense of well-being. This dissipated somewhat when I was given the total, but I left feeling that help was on its way.

We all long for a pill—preferably containing the ground-up root of some exotic plant—to help us lose weight, to guarantee us a long and healthy life, and to relieve stress. If not having enough time is the number-one complaint of working parents, feeling perpetually stressed out can't be far behind. When people feel a lot of stress, their behavior can become self-defeating. They begin to focus too much on the needs of others and stop caring adequately for themselves. They cut back on "low-priority" activities, even though these activities can buffer the impact of stress. The changes in lifestyle can be subtle and gradual, making it difficult for people to see that their behavior has changed. Yet this realization is vital; without it, the behavior modifications that will be discussed later in this chapter can seem unnecessary or trivial. "The Program"—if that is not too grand a term—capitalizes on the mundane and commonplace. It expects people to do almost nothing new; just rekindle old habits and build on what they already know.

The "Are You Ready for the Program?" Quiz

Even though the emphasis of this chapter is on making stress reduction as easy and enjoyable as possible, you will have to make a few small sacrifices. This totally untested, true-false quiz will help you decide if The Program is for you. Please rate each statement as either True or False:

- Science will soon confirm the healing powers of the hot fudge sundae.
- The lack of pleasure and fun in my life fulfills my need to be punished.
- Driving everywhere reduces the problem of congestion on our sidewalks.
- I don't have to worry—my uncle smoked like a chimney, drank like a fish, and ate like a pig, and he lived to be thirty-six.
- Living on the couch reduces the risk of sports-related injuries.
- The hundreds of studies relating exercise to stress reduction don't impress me; I'm not the kind of person to draw hasty conclusions.
- A coffee and donut on the drive to work reduces road rage.
- My life would be empty without the hassle and aggravation of coping with my work and family responsibilities.

If you have agreed with any of these items, I want you to know I fully sympathize, but you may want to skip to the next chapter.

Stopping the Vicious Cycle

I have used the following checklist on a number of occasions in stress management workshops. It was constructed on the basis of the common lifestyle changes that accompany stress. Compared to the time when you did not have to balance home and work, how often do you:

	More	Same	Less
Read just for interest and enjoyment	❑	❑	❑
Spend leisure time with your partner at home	❑	❑	❑
Take a *leisurely* walk	❑	❑	❑
Call a friend just to chat or whine	❑	❑	❑
Laugh	❑	❑	❑
Listen to music	❑	❑	❑
Spend time with family members you like	❑	❑	❑
Do absolutely nothing (and not feel guilty)	❑	❑	❑
Watch a favorite television show	❑	❑	❑
Take a nap	❑	❑	❑
Have fun playing with your child	❑	❑	❑
Do something new and different	❑	❑	❑

	More	Same	Less
Laugh really hard	❏	❏	❏
Sit and think about the positives in your life	❏	❏	❏
Make love	❏	❏	❏
Take time just for yourself	❏	❏	❏
Get together with your best friend	❏	❏	❏
Exercise	❏	❏	❏
Give yourself a reward or treat	❏	❏	❏
Take up a hobby	❏	❏	❏

My experience has been that the vast majority of people put almost all of their check marks in the "less" column. I frequently complete the checklist myself to see how I am doing. Rather than disclose my latest score, let me just say that, while I believe I am getting there, I must never forget to practice what I preach.

Contrary to many people's expectations, taking care of ourselves does not have to be overly time consuming, and it can become a regular part of our lives again. The focus here will be on activities that are neither new nor complicated. This is critical. Having to work hard at learning to reduce stress makes no sense when you are already feeling stretched to your limit. One of the principles of the program, therefore, is that learning is kept to a minimum. The price you pay for adopting this principle is that the program fails miserably when it comes to the glamor department. There's no stunning discovery, and I have deliberately omitted potential items that would require extensive time or effort. To give you one example, there have been studies of the psychological benefits of ballroom dancing. That's just fine for those who can rhumba but is no help to the rest of us. My mother had very definite and unshakeable ideas as to what young men had to learn, and ballroom dancing was one of them. My stint at the Guy Hayward School of Dancing is remembered as one of the most traumatic experiences of my childhood. Just hearing a few bars of a cha-cha triggers flashbacks and rekindles memories of weekly public humiliation. Even if you are more receptive to the implications of the research, you still have to find the time to attend a class. Then there's the question of where to practice. In the absence of a spatial home, where do you go? The back garden and the presence of understanding neighbors might work for some, although it would place a single parent at risk for committal. You will not have to wrestle with such issues if you sign up for The Program.

A note just for women is in order. It relates once again to the capacity for guilt. The chances of failing to follow through with any effort to reduce stress are higher for women than for men. For reasons that are almost incomprehensible, taking time for themselves can lead women to feel guilt.

In her recent article "What Makes Women Tired?", Donna Stewart and her colleagues at the University of Toronto spoke to this issue. They noted the relationship between women's lack of leisure time and work-family conflict. They attributed women's self-neglect to the drive to preserve an unrealistic and unnecessary image of what it means to be a mother. After presenting their data on the many reasons why women feel so tired and are especially vulnerable to depression, they concluded that "employed mothers with children may manage their parenting responsibilities in ways that do not damage their image of themselves as mothers, but they may do so at the expense of their own well-being by adopting a pattern of self-neglect to manage the multiple demands on their limited discretionary time."

I would never be so bold as to try to talk women out of guilt; after all, they are experts in the field and can generate guilt faster than I could ever hope to provide an antidote. The only thin ray of hope is to present the argument that taking care of themselves will allow them to do the best possible job as parents. It's like those safety videos on airlines—parents put on the oxygen mask first and then help their child.

Robert Thayer at California State University has studied a number of women and men to determine what they do to cope with stress. He and his colleagues have also examined which strategies work best for which purposes—be it overcoming a bad mood, boosting energy, or reducing tension.

Thayer divides activities into a number of categories. Some are active, such as exercise, specific relaxation techniques, and positive thinking. Others are passive; watching television, eating, resting, and sleeping. A third category involves our relationships with people who provide support and allow us to vent. Yet another focuses on distracting and pampering ourselves. His findings, as well as those from numerous other studies, tell us that a wide range of simple, everyday activities can be effective in making our lives more relaxed and enjoyable.

I have not listed all of the activities and strategies that emerge from the studies. Rather, I have chosen those that are the most universal and have the greatest potential to reduce the stress common among working parents.

Exercise—No Sweat!

My wife cannot believe that I have the nerve to write about exercise. She pointed out that credible authors have usually had at least some experience in the field. I have to admit that the last time I broke a sweat was when the air conditioning malfunctioned. I also grew up with a deep aversion to any activity that required gross motor skills. Being picked last for a team was a relief—it was reassuring to know that my teammates' expectations of me matched my talents. Being in the middle of a rugby scrum was my confirmation that *Lord of the Flies* accurately portrays the savage and primitive forces that can be aroused in even well-bred school children. I was lambasted for not running after the ball, but I simply did not want it. As far as I was concerned, it was reasonable and generous on my part to let someone else have it. The pinnacle of my school athletic career was placing second in an egg-and-spoon race at the age of nine. Then there was horseback riding. In addition to the indignities of ballroom dancing, my mother required that my brother and I take riding lessons. I asked her why she had found yet another way for me to prove that I was completely devoid of athletic ability. She reminded me that back in the days of the Persian Empire—which she assured me had been second only to ours—the three most important goals for young boys were to ride, to shoot, and to tell the truth. I wanted to suggest that we work on the truth-telling stuff first, but I knew we were not in negotiable territory.

Before you close the book in despair, let me try and convince you that I am, in fact, more qualified to talk about the type of exercise needed for this program than the muscle-bound jocks of the world. Such folks would certainly not find me credible, but they don't need to listen to me anyway. They already belong to fitness clubs and line up to subject themselves to the torture of treadmills, stationary bicycles, and cross trainers. They take pride in pushing their heart rates to 150, and even more pride in having a resting heart rate below 60. If my heart ever dropped that low, I would assume I was about to pass on. It's not that I haven't tried the regimented route; a few years ago a local fitness club had a recruitment drive and offered a twelve-month membership at a bargain basement price. I handed over my money and can still recall how fresh and energized I felt walking home with the membership card in my wallet. And that's where it stayed for the next year—I never set foot in the place again.

I am not trying to discourage people from joining the ranks of those who pack exercise classes and help sports leagues thrive—if you can develop the motivation and interest to become involved in new athletic pursuits, you are to be envied and congratulated. But this leaves the question of how to deal with those of us who "hit the wall" before we have run a block and whose motivation begins to dissipate as soon as we start tying up our running shoes. We need serious help.

The first question is this: does exercise really add to the quality of life, or is this proposition part of a huge plot driven by the greed of international sportswear conglomerates? I regret to say that there is no evidence to support the latter view. There is, however, an abundance of evidence proving that exercise does relieve stress.

The "doing what comes naturally" principle is the salvation; build on what you normally do, or have done in the past, rather than trying to radically change your activities and routines. Walking, bike-riding, and gardening are examples. Walking, in particular, has earned status as the most available, least expensive, and by far the easiest form of exercise to reduce stress and tension. It has instant appeal—it does not require any training, and barring injury or physical disorder, all of us have been walking for as long as we can remember. Even before that, we learned how to walk with minimal thought or planning. Even though you could sell tickets for a baby's first steps, it's really not an achievement. It is simply maturation; they are programmed to do it. Feed them and water them, and sooner or later they will get up and walk.

The main point is that walking is a normal part of our lives. It does not entail flaunting one's lack of talent or enduring self-inflicted pain. In passing, I should mention that there have been books written about walking. I browsed through one not so long ago; it was bursting with pictures and illustrations about topics such as body posture and arm position. No doubt there will be a sequel finally revealing the secret of that age-old dilemma—how to walk and chew gum at the same time. Do not feel that you have to study such books before you proceed; to my mind they belong among titles such as *Scratching for Beginners* and *Nose-Blowing Made Easy*.

Assuming that you feel confident enough about your walking skills, it is surprising how easy it is to increase the amount of time you devote to this activity. Here are a few examples:

Increasing Your Walking Time

- Pick the parking spot furthest away from the shopping mall entrance. Such a strategy has two advantages. The first, of course, is that it makes you walk further. The second is that it avoids the stress and aggravation that go along with trying to get the parking spot closest to the mall entrance. Picture two scenarios at the parking lot of a shopping mall just before Christmas. You cruise around the prized positions, searching for the first sign that a vehicle is about to leave. Of course, you are not the only predator, and your competitiveness will turn to paranoia and rage if you see someone attempting to take the spot that is rightfully yours. The people about to drive out of the parking spot do nothing to help the situation. In fact, they like to stir it up. Social psychologists have a knack for studying these odd quirks of human behavior. One researcher timed how long it took people to leave a parking spot after they had opened the car door. On average, drivers who were aware that someone was waiting to drive into their spot took longer to leave than those who did not spy anyone waiting in the wings. So much for joy to the world. The researchers attributed this phenomenon to primitive territorial behavior coupled with passive-aggressive tendencies.

Now picture this: you take a leisurely drive to the outermost region of the parking lot, find a spot with ease, and walk briskly towards the entrance. On your way you pass the stream of prowling motorists who are willing to spend ten stress-filled minutes finding a parking spot in order to save themselves a four-minute walk. Just in case you are thinking that an eight-minute round-trip walk is no big deal, remember that those little bits really do add up.

- While we are on the subject of shopping malls—plan to go to the entrance furthest away from the stores you intend to visit. The advent of super malls has meant that going from one end to the other is quite a jaunt. Believe it or not, articles have been written on the merits of "mall-walking." It is ideal for those who do not care to walk outdoors in inclement weather. It can be safer than walking alone and less physically demanding for those who have medical problems that affect physical stamina. Of course, it can be a favored activity among those who love to shop. Kathy, who once defined the Great Outdoors as the space between shopping malls, has been a die-hard mall-walker for many years.

- Create opportunities to walk. Take milk and bread off the supermarket shopping list—walk to a corner store to buy them as needed; take the stairs rather than the elevator; routinely get off one stop before the subway station nearest to your work; always walk to the mailbox.
- Set aside a small amount of time to ensure that you are walking regularly. Once around the block before going to bed can provide a few minutes of much-needed peace and quiet, as well as alleviating stress and improving sleep.

Sweating is entirely optional and has never been on my list of personal goals—a "good sweat" is the best example of an oxymoron I have come across. It is important, however, that anyone observing you would be able to detect signs of movement; a "brisk" walk is also better than the less energetic "stroll."

Let me emphasize that I have evidence to support my view that exercise does not have be synonymous with pain and suffering. I immediately warmed to Abby King when she concluded that vigorous exercise was not an essential requirement for experiencing psychological benefits. She and her colleagues at the Stanford University School of Medicine evaluated the effects of home-based and group exercise on the well-being of sedentary men and women. As predicted, exercise led to significant reductions in stress. Furthermore, a brisk walk outside or on a treadmill was every bit as effective as more vigorous forms of exercise.

A number of researchers, including King, have noted that home-based exercising is particularly effective, which is welcome news for those who would find it hard to accommodate fitness classes within their budgets or schedules. People are also more likely to stick with a program when it is self-directed and home-based. At the same time, high-frequency prompting (a fancy term for well-meaning but persistent nagging) helps sustain motivation. When I read the study that reached this conclusion, I was reminded of our youngest child. Alexandra knows that exercising is not my forte.

She also has made it clear that she wants me to be around long enough to be a grandparent to her children. My excursions around the neighborhood have become known as "grandpa walks," and her mentioning that one is overdue stimulates enough motivation and guilt to get me outside.

Music

The view of music as a stress-reduction technique has immediate appeal. Nobody gets out of breath or works up a sweat when operating a stereo, and listening to music requires no training or natural ability. It is also highly accessible—it can be listened to with ease in any area of the home, while driving to and from work, and even when walking or riding the subway.

The idea that music is readily accessible is, of course, neither novel nor profound. The point I want to emphasize is that music is more than just entertainment or a way to pass the time. There is an abundance of evidence indicating that it can have a significant effect on measures of psychological and physiological stress.

The value of music in reducing stress has caught the attention of not only those interested in human well-being. Holstein cows in Japan, for example, seem much happier about their twice-daily trips to the automatic milking machine when elevator music is piped into the shed. And in Chicago, mice get quite relaxed and cuddly in response to easy-listening music. My all-time favorite, however, has to do with piglets. The Center for the Study of Animal Well-Being in Washington State wanted to see if music could reduce stress in piglets. Just to make sure the little guys were distressed, the researchers used the simulation of stressful farmyard procedures such as being restrained for castration. Music did not calm them down and I am not in the least bit surprised. It would take more than a few excerpts from the *Moonlight Sonata* to improve my mood if I found myself in their position.

As for humans, the stress-reduction powers of music have been studied in many contexts. Music soothes people in waiting rooms and reduces stress during dental procedures. It calms children during immunization and alleviates preoperative and examination stress. Even surgeons' stress levels decrease in response to music. It seems they are quite picky, though. Stress reduction is better when the surgeon is allowed to pick the music. My advice would be not to argue the point. Let them pick whatever they want and just hope you don't drift off to the sounds of *Mac the Knife* or *The First Cut Is the Deepest.*

Music's beneficial effects also justify the expense of a tape or a CD player in the car, given that self-selected music tends to work best. The next time you see a motorist singing along to music as he cruises down the highway, remind yourself that, however strange he might look, he is probably one of the safer drivers in the vicinity. Listening to music reduces stress among drivers in highly congested areas. This is a good thing—the combination of high congestion and stress is known to be a factor contributing to many accidents.

I love the ingenuity of researchers when it comes to measurement. My favorite in the music and stress category is the study in which the researchers went so far as to collect saliva samples from singers during a public performance of one of Beethoven's choral works. These samples allowed them to measure chemical secretions related to stress. Unfortunately, I have only been able to secure a summary of the research study. I would love to see the full document just to find out how they actually collected the samples. Did the singers take turns using specimen cups when they had a few bars off, or did they expectorate in unison during the finale?

Just for the Fun of It: Laughter and the Pleasure Principle

The pleasure principle has to be one of Freud's greatest ideas. He recognized that the quest for pleasure is an inescapable human drive. Then he spoiled the party by coming up with the "super-ego," whose role is to help people get serious. This part of his theory will not be discussed any further, and I want you to know that, if you sign up for The Program, you will never hear the phrase "No pain, no gain."

It is hardly surprising that there is a link between doing things we enjoy and our mood. In fact, this link explains one of the causes of depression—people who are depressed tend to stop doing things that would bring them pleasure and improve their mood.

People have become quite serious about laughter; there is nothing even remotely humorous to be found in journals such as the *International Journal of Humor Research*. But while dissecting laughter tends to make it a lot less funny, the findings can be interesting. Laughter, for example, reduces the level of chemicals associated with stress, boosts the autoimmune system, and defuses conflict and feelings of hostility.

Rod Martin at the University of Western Ontario had people complete a daily laughter record. Just in case you did not know, the average person laughs eighteen times a day, although there is a considerable range. At the terminally miserable end of the scale, there are folks who never laugh at all. By contrast, there are those who never seem to take life seriously and laugh up to eighty-nine times per day. My initial reaction was to ask myself if we really care, but the fact that the experience of humor varies so much does lead to a relevant question: does the amount that people laugh have any impact on how vulnerable they are to stress?

"Is Laughter the Best Medicine" was the title of a paper by two researchers at the School of Social Sciences in Bath, England. Suzanne Skevington and Alison White studied patients suffering from chronic arthritis and found that those who were adept at finding something to laugh about in spite of their physical problems were better able to cope. There have also been workshops on the use of humor in therapy; at times, it can make it easier to deal with personal, distressing issues. More generally, laughter has a "stress-buffering" effect—it can reduce the extent to which people are affected by the stress in their lives.

One of the exercises I have used in workshops is to ask people to write a list of twenty simple, available things they know they enjoy doing but have allowed to become infrequent or extinct. You would be amazed at what some people would choose to do in the privacy of their homes. Most, however, come up with a very simple list: having a cup of tea; eating a favorite snack; reading for ten minutes; taking a hot, scented bath; writing a letter: doing a crossword; watching the news; surfing the Internet; and doing housework. You might wonder how that last item made the short-list. I am not suggesting that the Victorian writers who considered household duties to be "blessing" were onto something. I am also not contradicting what I suggested in Chapter 4 about cutting corners. The type of housework that has made the "just for pleasure" list is in a class of its own. It's that job you have ignored for so long but are now itching to do. It's cleaning that drawer or cupboard that has been upgraded from cluttered to disgusting, or arming yourself with rubber gloves and antibacterial spray while you tackle the farthest reaches of the fridge. My personal favorite is behind, rather than in, the fridge. The scene defies description; all I can say is that it is definitely not a pretty sight. A few minutes of hard scrubbing and scraping, however, restores a sense of hygiene, cleanliness, and safety to the kitchen. This illustrates the key point in order for a household task to make the list—it must yield dramatic results in a short period of time.

Nutrition

Nutrition has an odd status on the list of stress-reducing activities. Eating a favorite food is a common source of enjoyment and relaxation. The fact that people may not choose something that is of great nutritional value is unlikely to matter in most situations. However, if you find yourself carrying around a bag of donuts "just for medicinal purposes," the disadvantages of poor nutrition and the risks associated with comfort eating will have to be faced.

I find self-discipline in this area to be nothing short of torture. I would love to start each day with a pot of coffee and a cinnamon bun. I don't care what you add to it, how you dress it up, or how strong the data happen to be regarding its benefits, bran is bran, and the prospect of eating it first thing in the morning does nothing to brighten my day. But, the truth must be faced. While the occasional forbidden fruit is warranted on the basis of the pleasure principle, it should not become a regular item.

Stress can lead people to adopt counterproductive eating habits. At one extreme, there are people who react by not eating as much as they should. Skipping breakfast, for example, makes no sense—it's like starting the drive to work with a fuel gauge on empty. Then there are those who develop the habit of comfort eating; food makes them feel a whole lot better, at least in the short term. A general pattern of healthy eating that includes regular, balanced meals is needed to combat stress.

Rest, Sleep, and the Power Nap

Not long ago I read an article on the cumulative effects of lack of sleep. The message was simple—it is much harder to catch up than you might think. Sleeping in on your days off is probably not going to be enough. Over time, the body's energy supply gets depleted, and we often find ourselves running at a permanent deficit. This is a major reason why chronic fatigue is so common among working parents.

Sleep and rest are high on the list of passive activities that can alleviate stress and boost energy. One obstacle to overcome, however, is the notion that being able to get by on only a few hours' sleep is somehow a good thing. This idea that running yourself into the ground is a sign of dedication and good character goes along with the "culture of overwork" that plagues so many of today's parents. Putting your feet up and drifting into a semi-comatose state for ten minutes after supper—now *that* is a good thing, as is setting a latest permissible bedtime, no matter what task has to be left for later or abandoned. And taking twenty minutes to nap in the car during your lunch break is not a sign of weakness, although an alarm watch is recommended for the purposes of job security. Anyone determined to dust off that excuse about not having enough hours in the day to rest properly is referred back to the chapter on time management.

Friends, Neighbors, Lovers, and Pets

One aspect of the vicious cycle is that the more people feel strapped for time, the more inclined they become to jettison their social lives. They spend less time with friends, sometimes allowing the relationships to fade completely. Siblings and members of the extended family who used to get regular telephone calls are now neglected. The partners in a two-parent family may be married, but if you were to record the amount of time actually spent together, you might wonder why they bothered.

The benefits of having social relationships both within and outside the family are beyond dispute. The research is voluminous and goes beyond subjective measures of stress and fatigue. Having someone who will lend a sympathetic ear while you vent or offer a shoulder to cry on when you need it boosts your immune, endocrine, and cardiovascular systems, and makes you feel a whole lot better.

The contact does not have to be extensive. The subjects of Thayer's studies, for example, might simply call a friend for a quick chat or snatch a few moments with their spouse. Yet, seeking social support ranked high among the activities that made them more relaxed and energetic.

The decline that can occur in the quality of the marriage when both partners are employed is a major cause for concern given that the marital relationship plays a major role in buffering stress. The problem is not dwindling romance. While I am all for romance, sociologists tell us that it gets people into a lot of trouble. The more couples are caught up in an idealized, romantic view of marriage, the greater their dissatisfaction as the relationship progresses. This does not mean that the key to a successful marriage is to view it as the worst decision you have ever made and to expect it to be as exciting and rewarding as filling out a tax return. It's just that it is a rare couple that can sustain a relationship built primarily on romance.

The problem has more to do with the support system a good marriage supplies. Sociologists talk about couples needing to make the transition from romantic to conjugal love. This means that you come to terms with the fact that it is only in the world of romance movies and novels that Mr. Right exists without annoying mannerisms, a sagging waistline, or morning breath. Conjugal love is stable and becomes a central part of each partner's social support system. It gets them through the hard times and is characterized more by respect, understanding, and affection than by passion. Its focus is more practical than idealistic, and its rewards come from a sense of accomplishment in being able to work together and support one another.

I do not believe that couples have to resign themselves to a relationship that is all work or that passionate thoughts or hormonal surges should be promptly suppressed. I clearly remember watching my clinical supervisor working with a couple while I was a family therapy trainee. Libby always went straight to the point, but her directness was matched by the concern she communicated for their relationship. Her question, "With all the time you spend looking at the children, do you ever have eyes for each other?" highlighted an issue that had been long neglected by the couple. She prescribed a remedy; one was to call the other for a date. They were to go to a restaurant or coffee shop on their own, and the first person to talk about the children would pay the bill. People rarely messed with Libby—she earned and commanded much respect—but this was a prescription the couple had a great deal of pleasure filling.

Single parents, in particular, are at risk for feeling increasingly lonely and isolated. Furthermore, the parent's emotional well-being can have a profound impact on the family as a whole. Something as simple as maintaining or re-establishing ties with the extended family, for example, can ease feelings of loneliness, which, in turn, can increase the effectiveness of parenting. Ronald Taylor and his fellow researchers at Temple University reported that "kinship support" helped single parents to maintain more democratic styles of parenting, which had predictably positive effects on the adjustment of their children. For those parents who do not have a supportive extended family, reconnecting with friends can meet the same need.

I am not sure if I would have taken an article on the stress-reduction properties of dogs too seriously if it had not been for one of those remarkable coincidences that occur from time to time. Within days of reading the article, I found myself talking to a woman who was trying to decide if she could continue in her marriage of eighteen years. For many reasons, her relationship with her husband had deteriorated, leaving her doubtful that it would ever improve. At one point, she told me that her main reason for staying was their pet dog. "Sammy" was a very important part of her life. He was always happy to be with her, never hesitated to show affection, and was easy to please. She could always count on him, and she never had to worry that he might want another owner. While she did not expect a "custody" dispute should the marriage end, she knew she would be forced to move into a small apartment where Sammy would no longer have the run of the backyard while she worked. She could not imagine changing his life in this way and anticipated that she would postpone leaving her husband until Sammy died.

The article took on more meaning after this interview. Karen Allen and her research colleagues at Buffalo State University investigated the extent to which the presence of either friends or dogs alleviated stress in women. Having the opportunity to be with their pets was found to be especially beneficial, as measured by the women's physiological responses in a stressful situation. Allen discussed the importance of the pet's "nonevaluative social support"; they never pass judgment and cannot offer that well-meaning advice you really do not want. They have mastered the art of just being there.

Allen also reviewed other studies. She found, for example, that pet owners make fewer trips to the doctor and have a higher survival rate after discharge from a coronary care unit. In the latter study, the presence of a pet was more beneficial than a spouse. Just in case you are wondering, most pet stores will not let you trade in your husband for a puppy. You also have to be a pet lover to begin with; the women in Allen's study talked about their dogs as family members. In keeping with the comments made during my interview with Sammy's owner, a number remarked that, while husbands may come and go, and children eventually leave, a dog is forever.

The Spice of Life

Nuns have made excellent subjects for research. They are very accommodating when they have an opportunity to contribute, and they also tend to stay put, avoiding the attrition problems that plague so many longitudinal studies. The study involving nuns that I found intriguing concerned the effects of different types of activities on brain deterioration. Apparently, one of the early signs of Alzheimer's is the appearance of plaques, which are structural abnormalities of the brain's nerve cells. One order of nuns, who had agreed to donate their brains to research, was found to have a significantly lower incidence of these plaques than would be expected for their age at death. One aspect of their lives differentiated them from other orders studied. Although they had a specific mission, they were encouraged to become involved in a broad range of activities, often in the community. It was not uncommon for an elderly sister to take up a new hobby or pursue an interest that had been neglected for years. The hypothesis that the key to their more resilient brains was the fact that they had been stimulated in many different ways received support from other studies. Apparently, more of the same old thing does not work. A history teacher who decides to read more history books will not give his brain the boost it needs. A course in Thai cooking would, however, suffice—presumably because it will activate otherwise dormant brain cells. In keeping with my promise that new skills are not essential for the program, simply picking up a cookbook and trying new recipes would do the trick. All that matters is that you are doing something outside your normal range of activities.

Thinking Straight

How stressed people become is determined not only by their nature but also by how they think about, or interpret, a situation. Many years ago, I read *A Guide to Rational Living* by Albert Ellis. The book had a great deal of influence on my thinking as a psychologist and helped me become aware of how much power lies hidden in the way we think. If it is only the situation that causes us to feel stressed, then we are essentially helpless unless we can remove ourselves. However, if the way we think about the situation influences our emotions, then it becomes reasonable to consider how we might modify our thinking to reduce the level of stress.

Let me use an example to illustrate the point. I love camping. For close to twenty years, we have had an annual "Dads and Kids" camping trip. Eight of us take our children off for a week. The kids seem to love it, and the older ones keep coming back as adults. We have the odd rule or two, but no one cares if you want to roast marshmallows for breakfast, and behaviors such as brushing your hair and making sure your clothes match are seen as nothing short of neurotic.

Compare this to Kathy's view of camping. One year in the distant past, she joined us for the latter part of the week. I will have to give you my version of what transpired as Kathy still refuses to talk about it. She noticed things that had never even entered our minds. She became almost obsessed with the prevalence of "grit." She found it on the picnic table, in the food, and waiting for her every night in her sleeping bag. She could not understand why such primitive washing facilities were known as "comfort stations," and she seemed dismayed at the fact that her clothing reeked of campfire smoke. She woke on the last morning having suffered the additional indignity of a wet sleeping bag (it was really nothing more than a minor leak). As she crawled out of the tent to begin packing for home, she remarked, "I'd rather be in labor." She has yet to return.

Where did things go wrong? After all, the realities of camping were the same for Kathy as they were for the assembled masses at Dads and Kids. What made the difference was the way we thought about the excursion. Ellis would refer to these thoughts as our "self-statements." For the children, such self-statements might be, "Camping gives us a lot of freedom," "Great! We can see our summer friends," or "Perhaps we can beat the camp record for clam diving." Kathy's, on the other hand, might be, "Why did we bother coming out of the caves just to pay money to suffer the privations of prehistoric times," or "Why would I want to give up three days of my vacation to sit through a two-and-a-half-hour talent show watching my husband and his friends give their rendition of the Three Amigos singing *My Little Buttercup*"?

Two types of self-statement are particularly relevant. The first is what Ellis refers to as "awfulizing"—the ability some of us have to see the downside of any situation. I like to ask workshop participants to think of awfulizing examples, after which we all try to come up with more positive thoughts. Such positive self-statements need to be realistic; there's no point pretending that things are better than they really are. Here are a few examples from my last workshop:

Exercise: Thinking Positive

Awfulizing Thought	Positive Thought
There's absolutely no way I can get it all done today.	I have accomplished a lot—the rest will just have to wait.
Why do I never have any time to myself?	The children don't smell that bad—*I'm* playing in the bath tonight.
I just can't seem to cope these days.	I have two great kids and a steady job—I must be doing something right.
This house is an absolute mess.	My in-laws aren't scheduled for a visit this week.
I promised to help decorate her room months ago.	I'll let her know I haven't forgotten—sooner or later we'll find the time.

The second type of negative self-statement has to do with the unwritten rules we have for our lives. Ellis argues that a number of these rules are unnecessary and serve only to generate guilt and stress. Such thoughts often contain or imply the words "should" or "must." Again, let me illustrate with examples from the same workshop:

Unwritten-Rule Thought	Positive Thought
I *must* get to the grocery store tonight.	If having no cereal for breakfast is the worst thing in our lives tomorrow, we are truly blessed.
I *should* be able to get more done.	Says who?
I *must* get this finished tonight.	I formally resign as Superwoman.
I *have to* get more organized and efficient.	It would be better if I could finish it tonight, but there may not be enough time.
I *should* be spending more time with the children.	Right now, finishing this project is my priority; I'll make sure we have a family day on the weekend.

At times it may seem that simply modifying the way we think is pointless; after all, the reality of the situation does not change. One counterargument is that our *thoughts* about the situation are, in fact, the reality. Not being a philosopher, I do not feel qualified to expand on this line of reasoning, so I will revert to the social scientific mode. In Robert Thayer's study about coping with stress, subjects found that concentrating on how they were thinking about situations was the most effective way of countering fatigue. It was also one of the common ways in which people reduced tension and improved their mood. Such benefits can go a long way in combating the work-family conflict. Something to think about.

The Art of Doing Absolutely Nothing

Several years ago in an attempt to overcome my midlife crisis I signed up for Outward Bound. Participants spent two weeks in the wilderness pretending that rappelling down rock faces and getting tangled in rope courses thirty feet up in the trees were more fun than anyone deserved to have. We went on a five-day canoe trip and were eaten by blackflies on every portage and soaked by the wind and rain when we finally managed to escape onto the lake. As for the food, I never want to see another plate of bulgur. To top it all off, you pay a large sum of money for the privilege of participating.

In spite of all the suffering, it was a remarkable two weeks. One of the most memorable experiences was the "solo." Each of us was abandoned on our own small section of shoreline, far enough apart so that we could neither see nor hear one another. And there we sat for three days, hoping that the leaders were serious when they said they would come back. I learned afterwards that some people kept themselves busy building shelters and exploring their territory. Lacking their drive and ambition, I did nothing. The feeling of being still, quiet, and peaceful became almost hypnotic. I fasted— this seemed much more sensible than preparing food—and my daily routine did not extend beyond a swim in the lake. The time flew by, and I cannot recall ever feeling more relaxed and content.

There are how-to books on almost every topic, but none has tackled the art of doing nothing—I suppose anyone qualified to write the book would never get around to it. I have a good friend who runs a successful and expanding company. Rick seems driven at times and recognizes his need not to become overwhelmed by the demands of his work and family life. I recently adopted one of the daily rituals that he rarely allows to be displaced. In spite of indications that his staff are wondering if he has finally lost it, he closes his office door, ignores everybody, and meditates for fifteen minutes. He slows himself down, focuses on what is truly important in his life, and then clears his head completely. It would be very easy for Rick to find another use for those fifteen minutes—there's always something that needs to be done. But he is convinced that this time is a worthwhile investment rather than a waste; what's more, it makes him feel good. Of course, being the boss is an advantage; coming to work and announcing your plan to start the day by doing absolutely nothing would be a career-limiting decision for many people. My version of the ritual is to get up before the rest of the family and spend my fifteen minutes concentrating on the peace and quiet around me.

I do not pretend to understand the complexities of meditation. Our son, Tim, has studied this art for years and sometimes spends days at a time meditating. While simpler and less time-consuming approaches do not offer the same depth of experience, they are remarkably effective in reducing the impact of stress. They are utilized in treatment programs for anxiety and are also incorporated in many relaxation tapes. Listening to one of these tapes can be a good introduction to the art of doing nothing; it provides structure and helps keep you on track.

Putting It All Together

I like to devote the last part of the workshops to developing a self-care plan for coping with the stress that is such an inherent part of the conflict between work and home. There's no universal prescription—each person needs a tailor-made plan—but over the years I have found the following two-step format to be effective.

Step 1: Referring back to the checklist on pages 92 to 93, select five items that you would most like to move to the "same" or "more" category. In making the selection, decide which activities are most likely to benefit you. Although all are effective, each individual will have a preference. Some people respond best to the more active forms of stress management, for example, while others favor the passive approach.

Step 2: Write down ways of incorporating the five items into your week. Be creative. You may need to earmark time for getting together regularly with a friend or picking up a video from the comedy section in preparation for a family movie night.

Others, however, can be combined with existing activities. Mall-walking is an example, as are listening to your favorite music on the drive home or making sure that your daily menu includes at least one treat.

Small, simple changes are easier to implement and sustain than the major transformations we promise ourselves on New Year's Day and abandon within the week. Without realizing it, our lives can gradually become stripped of those things that protect and support us. Reinstating them can be fun; it can also be beneficial—for ourselves and those who work and live with us.

Taking Care of Our Children: Parenting Styles

There will always be days when we think of being childless as a golden but missed opportunity. Our children may be wonderful, but they can also be unreasonable, demanding, and bewildering—just like we probably were at their ages. No one expects that raising children will be hassle free, but the challenges they bring can be a major factor adding to the work-family conflict. The effectiveness of our parenting will, therefore, have a strong impact on our ability to balance work and home. Our parenting influences how children will respond to day care and helps determine the adjustment of latchkey children. It also predicts the degree to which children develop self-reliance—a valuable characteristic when they are needed to make a contribution to the day-to-day running of the family. A positive approach to parenting allows chores and responsibilities to be negotiated and assigned in a way that ensures that parents feel in charge, and their children feel listened to and respected. Above all, research in this area reassures us that while we may devote much of our time to work—and in spite of the fact that others may become involved in caring for our children—we retain a great deal of influence in their lives.

The Nature of the Job

There is something unique about being a parent. Somehow, it remains extremely popular in spite of the fact that it offers no pay, no promotions, and no thanks. In a desperate effort to gain at least some appreciation, parents have created Mother's Day and Father's Day. I suppose one day off each year is a beginning, but we're not exactly a tribute to the labor movement.

The job of parenting is also very demanding and requires a great deal of skill. We begin with responsibility for a totally dependent infant. We are supposed to know what she needs and how to provide it, even though she has very limited ways of communicating. We eventually end up with responsibility for a teenager, who insists she is dependent on us for nothing but is saving us from loneliness by continuing to grace us with her presence. We are supposed to know how to make this experience successful and how to live with the fact that she now has far too many ways of communicating exactly what she thinks, feels, and wants.

My own career as a parent began thirty-four years ago. The question of why I still have a house full of children as young as eleven keeps me awake at nights and bewilders my friends who are already enjoying the empty nest. I like to tell my children that I had a large family in the hope that sooner or later one would turn out right, but they fail to find this even faintly amusing.

While being a parent may be a major part of our adult lives, we receive little, if any, training for the job. On the few occasions when I have time to engage in reflection, I wonder why I adopted a particular approach to raising my first two children. I also wonder why that approach has changed so much over the last three decades. l certainly cannot claim to have been consistent when it comes to child-rearing. I launched my career as parent when I was a twenty-year-old in the sixties. Family life was based on the belief that freedom of expression was all that was needed for children to grow in an atmosphere of peace and harmony. Joanne and Tim called me by my first name and were enrolled in a free school. Somehow they survived, in spite of the fact that they spent their early years in a single-parent home that was part hovel and part commune, surrounded by a cast of characters who were determined to suppress any potential they might have to become pillars of middle-class society. Fortunately, none were adopted as role models, and although structure, routine, and orderliness remained foreign concepts until the children were preteens, they managed to reach adulthood intact. By the time my next child was born, I was considerably older and, while not necessarily wiser, married to someone who never had so much as an inkling to write poetry or put flowers in her hair. Kathy and I are raising Aaron, Kiera, and Alexandra very differently. They call me "Dad" and attend regular schools. Their daily lives are predictable, and their clothes match. The search for domestic peace and harmony continues, but I am now willing to accept that a reasonable substitute can be procured through use of prolonged banishment to their rooms or, better still, a lengthy stay with a kindly and unsuspecting relative.

The changes in child-rearing style that have occurred in my own history as a parent do not necessarily represent improvements. Although I would not want to return to my earlier way of life, it's not only because I want to stay married to Kathy. It also reflects the fact that, as a parent in my fifties, I am a very different person than I was in my twenties. A similar lack of consistency can be found when I compare our current views and practices to those of our friends and relatives. Aaron, our green-vegetable hater, would tremble at the thought of trading places with his cousin who has to finish everything, including brussels sprouts. At five, Alexandra was permitted to go on sleepovers (encouraged would be more accurate) but had a friend whose parents did not feel this type of separation was a good idea at such a young age. We and our friends and relatives do not always share the same views regarding discipline, and only some of us are highly selective when it comes to the movies and television programs our children watch. While some of our friends' children are quite adept at budgeting, Aaron, Kiera, and Alexandra have yet to receive a regular allowance.

Where's the Manual?

I have lost count of the number of parents I have met who have looked at their child and lamented, "He didn't come with a manual." Their hope, of course, is that I will happen to have one they can borrow. Over the years, there have been people in my field only too happy to oblige. They wrote with authority about the best and only way to raise a healthy, well-adjusted child. They often stated with equal authority that failing to follow the manual would condemn the child to become one of society's failures and misfits. I suspect that the main reason these manuals are hard to find today is that they were written primarily by men who had never so much as changed a diaper, dealt with a tantrum, or put a child to bed. They were also full of conviction and dogma but very short on field studies; many of the ideas were later found to be wrong, and a number proved to be harmful.

In the absence of a manual, parents must develop their own policies and procedures, and tailor them to the demands of balancing work and home. One source of information comes from our own experiences as children. On occasions, we will try to emulate the child-rearing practices of our own parents. At other times we may use our childhood experiences to decide what *not* to do. This determination may not always lead to success; old patterns have a habit of resurfacing. I remember vowing never to expose my children to repetitive lectures; I was given many in my youth because of my tendency to collect rather than overcome faults. But the temptation to use my offsprings' failings as a cue to sharing the vast expanses of my wisdom is irresistible. So far, they have hidden their admiration and gratitude behind a facade of scorn and indifference, but I am not deterred. I solemnly swore never, never to begin a sentence with, "When I was your age..." I lied.

Another source of information on child-rearing is the body of literature relating to parenting styles. In the 1970s, studies by psychologist Diana Baumrind sparked three decades of research into the effectiveness and long-term impact of differing approaches to child-rearing. The intention of the research was never to dictate what parents should do. Rather, it provided information that could be useful when trying to decide how to parent.

Baumrind's early work involved gathering information on child-rearing practices through direct observation of parents and their preschoolers. This type of research has since been extended to encompass older age ranges. Two dimensions of parenting emerged. One refers to the demands and standards established by parents and the efforts made to control their children and assert parental authority. The second is how responsive, sensitive, and accepting parents are in the way they relate to their children. I will discuss the three main parenting styles that have been described; each is a particular combination of the two dimensions.

Permissive Parenting

Permissive parents make relatively low demands on their children and are not big on control. They may, however, be very responsive and involved. They can be warm and loving, they pay attention to their children, and they value communication and open discussion.

The permissive approach can be related to the parents' fundamental beliefs about how the world should be run. My heroes as a first-time parent were still those songwriters and authors who wanted to topple the traditional hierarchies in society and turn the world into a global Woodstock. I spent a few years working diligently for the cause; while we may not have succeeded in the long run, we had a lot of fun trying. Like many other permissive parents, I did not want to encroach on my children's rights and freedoms; to do so would have seemed like selling out to the Establishment. As an adolescent, I had been told many times that I had an attitude problem; as a young parent, I had no intention of ever seeking treatment.

The permissive approach would be just fine if children knew what to do with all this freedom. But, they simply do not. Maturation may take care of some of the important things, such as motor development and speech readiness, but it will not produce a child who can be a joy to all around her. While it is true that we give our children license to act in ways that would not be acceptable in adulthood, we also seek to change their behavior. The expression "kids will be kids" allows us to simultaneously communicate our tolerance of what they do and our hope that they will eventually stop doing it. "It's just a stage," we say in an effort to reassure ourselves that maturation will give us at least some help in producing a well-adjusted adult.

The development of cooperation provides a good example. It simply is not a natural, instinctive way of behaving. If you want to watch raw, primitive violence, you do not have to tune into hockey. Just put two eighteen-month-olds in a room together devoid of play activities. Then introduce one highly desirable toy. I guarantee that you will not see behavior that communicates, "after you..." or "why don't we take turns?" What you are likely to witness would qualify as a blood sport, and attempts at peace-making are next to pointless unless you have a weakness for failure. The situation is not hopeless—as far as I know, there are no studies indicating that fighting over toys in toddlerhood predicts later incarceration. But you do have to be patient. A degree of maturation is required, but only so that the child can reach a stage of cognitive development where he can be *taught* the type of self-control and empathy required for cooperation. This teaching needs to go on for quite some time, probably because the child would love to revert to the primitive stage and take another run at making sure he always gets the toy first.

The key to learning cooperation is for the child to achieve a balance between his goals and his respect for the goals of the other person. There is another type of balance that is also critical—the balance between independence and compliance. In his book *No and Yes: On the Genesis of Human Communication*, Rene Spitz referred to the young child's willingness to say "no" to parents as "beyond doubt the most spectacular intellectual and semantic achievement during early childhood." That may be stretching it a bit, and I doubt there are too many parents who have celebrated the first time their child said "no" as a major milestone. The child's ability to assert herself, however, is an important part of becoming autonomous and independent. These are qualities we need to foster in our children unless it is our goal to keep them at home forever.

One of the risks of permissive parenting is that these types of balances are not achieved. Too much emphasis is placed on what the child wants at a particular moment; allowing him to express his own needs is not countered by efforts to make him sensitive to those of others. The parents may also be reluctant to counter the child's wish for autonomy. They want their child to express himself and be assertive, and worry that placing restrictions on behavior will stifle individuality.

It is important to emphasize that the parents can be very focused on the child and highly sensitive to her needs and feelings. The problem arises, however, when the child does not develop the level of cooperation and respect for rules, boundaries, and authority needed to be successful in broader social situations.

Although a permissive approach often reflects parents' views and beliefs, there are occasions on which it is more related to a lack of skill. Some parents find themselves unable to impose the type of discipline they believe their child needs. Their efforts to exert control may have led to recurrent conflict, and they become "battle-weary," throwing their hands up in despair. In some instances, they may indeed be raising a very challenging son or daughter; there are innate differences in temperament, as any parent with more than one child will have learned from firsthand experience. Whatever the reason, the parents feel unable to stop their child from behaving in ways they consider unacceptable.

A number of studies have examined the consequences of permissive parenting. The term "delayed socialization pattern" has been used to refer to the problems a child can encounter as she grows up. Children of permissive parents can be self-indulgent and impulsive. Their tendency to focus on themselves can cause them to become increasingly rebellious in situations in which there is an authority figure, such as the school environment. It can also have a negative effect on self-reliance. Although the parents may have hoped that freedom would provide the opportunity for growth and achievement, the opposite may prove to be the case. An overly permissive home environment entails a risk that the child will not have been provided with a clear sense of direction. He has not had the experience of working towards goals that were set for him by his parents and has missed this valuable opportunity to prepare for later independence.

Authoritarian Parenting

The authoritarian parent places a great deal of emphasis on control—responsiveness and acceptance are a distant second. They know how things should be done and expect obedience. Negotiation and discussion are not encouraged. From the parents' point of view, their authority should be accepted.

Authoritarian parenting conjures up images of the stereotypical "spare the rod and spoil the child" Victorian parent. I am prepared to confess, however, that there have been times when an authoritarian approach would make our family life much easier. Just a moment's thought will convince you that life at home would be much less complicated if your children considered it an honor to obey your every command and direction.

I also believe we need to recognize that we are, in effect, quite authoritarian in the way we raise very young children. Diaper changes, for example, are rarely a topic for negotiation. The toddler who has obviously made full use of his diaper is not greeted with, "Christopher, what would you like to do? Do you want to join us at the supper table and let it stew for a while, or would you like me to clean you up?" And thinking of mealtimes, how much choice does the nine-month-old get when it comes to the menu? I am convinced that the major motivation for children to develop the motor skills required for holding and directing a spoon is their wish to have at least some say over what is shoved into their mouths. Think back to occasions when you have witnessed children being fed in a high chair. It would not be uncommon for the menu to include slightly warmed, pureed squash. My traveling takes me to many parts of the world, but I have yet to encounter this dish on a menu. Undaunted, however, the parent manages to get a spoonful into the child's mouth. She, in response, does what any self-respecting human being would do—she spits it out. Undeterred, and with lightning speed and dexterity, the parent scoops the squash back into the spoon, reinserts it into the child's mouth, and adds a cheery, "Isn't this yummy?"

The reason we do not give young children much choice is that they are not yet capable of exercising it. Newborn children are entirely dependent on us for their survival. There is so much we have to do for them that we become, out of necessity, "benign dictators." We are required to exert a lot of control; while the principle of "natural consequences" has an important role later on in parenting, it does not apply when you see your child toddling towards the top of the stairs or reaching for a dangerous object.

It's useful to occasionally remind ourselves of how much control we exert. This emphasizes one of the main challenges of parenting—helping our children move from almost total dependency to the point in their lives where they can become independent members of society. In order to assist in this progression, parents must also undergo a great deal of change. We begin with almost 100 percent control over our children's lives. Over the course of their childhood, however, we need to reach the point where control is no longer necessary.

The authoritarian parent is one who fails to make this shift and probably does not believe the shift is necessary in the first place. A child's assertion of autonomy is construed as rebellion, and parental negotiation would be a sign of weakness. Not surprisingly, children raised in this type of environment can have problems with self-reliance. They have not had opportunities to develop their own decision-making skills. Some of the research findings indicate that they tend to be relatively withdrawn, fearful, moody, and irritable. Gender differences have also been reported. Girls tend to remain more passive and dependent during adolescence; boys, on the other hand, can react to the environment by becoming rebellious and aggressive.

Democratic Parenting

One of the hallmarks of democratic parenting is the balance between the parent's need to exert control and responsiveness to the child's need to become more independent and responsible. Such an approach appears to be effective for many families, particularly for those in which there is no full-time homemaker. One reason appears to be the combination of strong involvement and an emphasis on teaching children to be responsible and independent. Peace and harmony are by no means guaranteed, but the children are likely to acquire abilities and traits that make for a more cooperative and satisfying family life, which in turn reduces the negative spillover that contributes to the conflict between home and work.

The democratic approach may be a general parenting style, but it places a great deal of emphasis on responding to children in a highly individualized manner. The need for control provides an example. We have a son who rarely challenges limits and seems very capable of determining for himself what is and is not reasonable to do. He has a younger sister, however, who inherited all of my rebellious genes. I can still recall the struggle I had with Alexandra as a five-year-old when we were walking our bikes across a busy intersection. I had to physically bar her way when she attempted to ignore the crosswalk signal. I initially thought that we had somehow failed to teach her this aspect of survival, but I soon became aware that she fully understood the meaning of the signal. Her approach to the whole issue was summed up by a single comment. Pointing to the signal, she exclaimed, "I don't like people telling me what to do!" As much as we have applauded her determination and self-reliance, we also wish she would not keep her need for advice and direction so well-hidden. Drawing a line is tantamount to giving her the invitation to cross it, and I am counting on her adolescence to keep me alert and sharp as I traverse my fifties.

From Zero to One Hundred

Although they may not have thought about it in this way, most parents want to become redundant by the time their children reach the age of majority. Anyone with older children knows how quickly the time flies. It can seem like only yesterday that your hulking seventeen-year-old was a cute and adorable infant asleep in your arms. The need to teach our children to take control of their lives—and the relatively short period of time in which we must accomplish this task—dictates that we begin the process as early as possible. A gradual and planned transfer of power is likely to be far more effective than a more sudden and abrupt approach. It is probably not wise, for example, to keep adolescents on too tight a rein, only to suddenly cut them loose when they leave home. Chances are, they will not know what to do with themselves and will be back on your doorstep pleading for an extension on their childhood. Alternatively, they will treat their first real taste of freedom as license to have fun, take risks, and run wild while you look on aghast, wondering where you went wrong.

Control can be dealt with in three ways. The two extremes are the "because I said so approach" and the "it's up to you" approach. The authoritarian parent likes to perfect the first approach, while the permissive parent is enthusiastic about the latter. Before talking about the middle ground, I want to give these extremes their due. Not all issues should be negotiable. The list of non-negotiables will vary according to the parent's values, beliefs, and preferences. In our home, we have every intention of remaining inflexible when it comes to forbidding physical fighting between the children, skipping school, and underage drinking. We are not naive enough to believe we can always stop such behaviors from occurring, but we will never condone or ignore them. This aspect of parenting is similar to society's need for a legal system. There are some things that are deemed wrong and will not accepted, no matter how old you are.

I also suggest allowing parents the right to exercise a veto. There are times when negotiation and discussion seem to be getting nowhere and are simply becoming a waste of everyone's time. The judicious and occasional use of "because I said so" in response to your child's "why?" may not be recommended in most parenting books, but I see it as a coping skill essential to preserving what remains of my sanity. In similar fashion, the "it's up to you" approach is not exclusive to permissive parenting. To the contrary, its use should increase steadily over the course of childhood. The problem with permissive parenting, however, is the approach is employed before the child is able to cope with the added responsibility and freedom.

This brings us to the area between the extremes—the "let's work it out together" approach. This is where life becomes somewhat more complicated. Decisions need to be made jointly, and while this is a noble enterprise, there are many situations where it can be hard to get people to agree. The idea, however, is to give children the opportunity to voice their opinions and gradually assume more responsibility.

Democratic parenting is not about abdicating power and responsibility; rather, it is motivated by the wish to transfer power and responsibility to our children according to their readiness and stage of development. When I first began presenting on this topic, I focused almost exclusively on teenagers. Democratic parenting can, however, be a viable approach much earlier on. The issues will naturally be different. For teenagers, high-priority items are likely to include the amount of time they are free to be out with friends, curfews, homework, styles of dress, choice of friends and recreational activities, and attendance at family gatherings. With younger children, the issues can sound almost trivial. From the child's perspective, however, they are significant. Being able to have a say when it comes to which television programs you can watch, the chore you are to assume, the clothes you will wear, and how much of that foreign-looking vegetable you have to at least sample may not seem like a training ground for making decisions in the board room, but I believe it is. I also believe it is important to find something, however small, that we can allow young children to discuss and eventually decide for themselves.

Sometimes we think we are giving our children more choices than is probably the case. I was reminded of this many years ago when informing Aaron that it was his turn to do the dishes. Personally, I have never objected to taking my turn. The family rule is that the person doing the dishes picks the music, which guarantees that all of the children will quickly leave the facility as they see me reach for the CD case. I am left with fifteen minutes of peaceful listening and a task that is ridiculously easy to complete successfully. Of course, I have no intention of sharing this enthusiasm with other members of the family. They would just insist that allowing me to do their dishes would be an act of kindness. At age nine, Aaron would certainly have been happy to relinquish his turn. On the night in question, he was downstairs watching television. He was not exactly ignoring me, but by the time you reach the fifth repetition, "I'll be up in a minute" seems to lack sincerity. I became more insistent, only to be told that he was watching his "most favorite show." This would have been any show that happened to be on between seven in the morning and eight at night. Frustration eventually led me to exclaim, "Aaron, you have a choice! You can either get up here right now and do your dishes or the television goes straight off, there will be no snack, you will go straight to bed, and we will cancel all contributions to your education fund." Some choice!

The more we recognize that we start off parenting by giving children almost no choices, the more we can be sensitive to the need to find opportunities to transfer power and control—no matter how modest these opportunities may be. Such efforts may not guarantee peace and harmony, but they can create a healthy family atmosphere. Children learn that power can be given to them; they do not always have to fight for it. The importance of this realization was highlighted in a study by Judith Smetana at the University of Rochester. Smetana has a fascination for arguments between parents and adolescents, and the results of her studies have been illuminating. Assume, for example, that you are videotaping a teenager and her parents in a laboratory. You invite them to discuss a topic that has led to conflict in the home—perhaps curfews. You might think that the family would be on their best behavior, particularly as they are being taped. It could start off this way, but Smetana found that polite and restrained expressions of disagreement quickly gave way to a full-blown argument. The interesting part of the research was how the participants viewed the argument in hindsight. The parents focused on content; if the topic for debate had been their child's curfew, this specific issue was first and foremost on their agenda. Although this issue was also of interest to the adolescent, it was not the number-one priority. More often than not, the primary interest was something Smetana referred to as "jurisdiction." The adolescent wanted more control over her life. She might have been discussing curfews, but any other topic could have been the means to the same end.

Reading Smetana's studies gave me a flash of insight into the arguments we used to have with our oldest daughter. There would be times when we were hotly debating a particular expectation or rule. We would reach the point where there could be no doubt that we had presented an open-and-shut case. But Joanne was a pro. Just as we thought victory was ours, we would suddenly realize that we were no longer debating the original topic. Somehow she had managed to steer the discussion to a related, but different, issue; it was like trying to nail Jell-O to the wall. I now understand that our reasons for participating in the discussion were very different. Kathy and I were there to try to resolve a specific issue; Joanne just wanted to win.

The fact that children and adolescents want more power does not, of course, mean we should give it to them. More independence and control need to be earned. They may also be taken away if experience proves that greater parental guidance and input are still required.

Not Another Family Meeting

The democratic style requires a great deal of communication and negotiation in order to effect the balance between parental control and the child's growing independence. Whenever I think of communication, I'm forced to admit that I have mastered only half the process. I have absolutely no difficulty telling my children what I think. From my perspective, I am giving them the benefit of my infinite wisdom; from theirs, I am lecturing. Chances are, they could recite each lecture, chapter and verse. I am still working on the other half of the process—listening. Just as important as listening itself is the invitation to speak. The type of responsiveness that characterizes democratic parenting requires *asking* our children to tell us how they feel and think about matters.

Kiera once reminded me of our failure to invite her opinion. This time, it was her turn to do the dishes (somehow dishes always seem to be a major issue in our home). She was moaning and groaning and otherwise trying to convince us that doing dishes was a violation of her rights. I was about to give her one of my two standard replies. The first is "Tell someone who cares." This response may not be found in parenting books, but I use it when I am feeling tired, pressed for time, or just plain grumpy. The longer response is something like, "Kiera, you are absolutely right. Your mother and I are simply trying to help you deal with the fact that there are many injustices in the world. It is much better that you learn to cope with them here while you are young; this will prepare you to cope with life as you grow older. This is a wonderful learning experience for you—enjoy it." In a moment of weakness, however, I decided to allow her to sit down and explain why expecting her to do the dishes was not fair. After all, I had written about this aspect of communication in one of my books—perhaps some of the ideas actually worked. Kiera proceeded to present her case and I bit my tongue, vowing that I would resist the temptation to interject. She pointed out that she had to do dishes while her younger sister did not. Chores had been assigned when Alexandra was too young to assume such kitchen duties; she had been given a token job—helping to take the garbage out every week. Kiera pointed out that I always helped with this chore and that, even on the worst winter's day, it never took more than two minutes. Dishes took much, much longer—something akin to purgatory. I realized that it had been years since we had opened up the topic of chores for discussion. I was reminded of the need to provide frequent opportunities for the children to talk about family matters before they became a source of resentment. (I should add that the matter was resolved to Kiera's satisfaction. Alexandra, however, has yet to forgive her sister for her instigating her promotion to the kitchen staff.)

Democratic parents are like good employers. They want to listen to what you have to say and are open to change, even though they may not agree to it. Each person emerges from the discussion feeling listened to and respected. It is equally important for children to believe that their opinions and wishes have not been discounted, even if their requests meet with a definite "no." Whenever possible, adding a note of optimism and hope is desirable. The child who wants to ride the bus on his own and meet a friend at the movies may be told that he is too young for this type of independence. Explaining when this will be possible, and coming up with other ways in which he can have more freedom, can help him understand that what he wants is reasonable and eventually attainable.

Another important aspect of communication and negotiation is to be specific rather than general. Discussing principles and generalities can often get you nowhere fast. If you are blessed with a child who makes no distinction between chores and slavery, I am sure you have a well-rehearsed lecture that begins with, "You're part of this family too, don't you think it is only fair that you make a contribution?" Everything will be resolved in an instance if you are met with the response, "You are absolutely right. Why didn't I think of that before? Please give me extra chores so that I can demonstrate my commitment to the family." If you don't believe that you will be met with this type of response, it is probably far more productive to work towards specific goals than to embark on a debate about general principles of fair play. The goals need to be concrete—exactly what does he need to do to make a contribution?

Rules and Consequences

Theory says that children secretly want structure and discipline and are truly grateful when we provide them. The reason that this remains largely a theory is that it's hard to find children who will publicly support the claim. No self-respecting daughter would ever admit to wanting to be told "no" after asking to go to an all-night party, and I cannot recall even one occasion on which any of our five children has said, "By the way, I just wanted to say thank you for grounding me and taking away all my earthly privileges." While I believe children do appreciate discipline, they also resist it, and even though democratic parenting emphasizes understanding, there is ample room for imposing consequences when rules have been broken and lines crossed. This can also be an opportunity for discussion and negotiation. If parents invite their children to share the responsibility for decision-making, it is an easy matter to ask them to share the task of establishing consequences for not keeping to the rules they have helped make.

You might assume that if children are allowed to decide on the punishment for their crimes, the most severe would be no spinach for the rest of their childhood. My first two children spent several years attending a free school. The term "free school" was unfortunate; it conjured up images of teachers bound and gagged while the unruly masses finger painted on the walls. To the contrary, the school provided an organized and regulated learning environment. The students were nonetheless given a large part of the responsibility for establishing rules and consequences. The teachers did not typically try to persuade them of the need for discipline; rather, it was often the teachers' role to help them realize that being hung, drawn, and quartered was perhaps a bit of an overreaction to shoving a fellow student in the school yard. There was no messing with these youngsters. They knew they were setting rules that applied as much to themselves as to others. That knowledge did not stop them from establishing consequences for misbehavior that were guaranteed to have a real and negative impact on the offender.

I have met with many families over the years who are in the process of establishing rules. I cannot recall one occasion on which efforts to involve children in setting consequences were not at least partially successful. There was the sixteen-year-old who wanted to regain his mother's trust and knew that not skipping school was an essential condition. He successfully negotiated that, if he skipped once, he would hand over his collection of hockey cards for a month. An eight-year-old needed no more than a moment's thought to suggest that losing her bike for a week would be an appropriate consequence for failing to wear her helmet, which also impressed me.

The only suggestion I would add is to endeavor to make sure that the consequences are logical, short-lived, and concrete. If your daughter stays out later than agreed, having to sit at home next Friday evening helps repay the debt—and perhaps only one Friday night's internment is sufficient. Losing a right or privilege for months on end only encourages a sense of hopelessness that fosters resentment and rebellion rather than self-control. Lengthy discussions aimed at changing opinions, attitudes, or feelings can be an exercise in frustration. "Why did you agree to come in at twelve and not get back until one?" is about as logical a question as the judge asking "Why were you driving at eighty in the fifty zone?" Unless you are an obstetrician on your way to a multiple delivery, your answer is irrelevant. You have sinned, and you have no defense. Your daughter was probably doing no more than living for the moment and having the type of fun and excitement you can only envy. At some point, she may decide that giving in to impulse isn't worth the hassle. Until then, be kind to yourself. Mete out the punishment with a minimum of words, lessen your chances of a stress-related illness, and trust that the general trend will be upwards.

Impact of Democratic Parenting

Research in the social sciences can be frustratingly inconsistent at times; it is very hard to know what to believe when studies asking the same question come up with very different answers. From this perspective, the research into the effectiveness of democratic parenting is a welcome change. Diana Baumrind's early research, followed by many other studies in this field, yielded results that almost always pointed in the same direction—democratic approaches to parenting seemed to be the most effective.

Three studies serve to illustrate the findings. Susan Crockenberg at the University of Vermont and her co-researcher Cindy Litman at the University of California devised ways to study how parents exerted control over their young children. They were especially interested in how parents responded to the word "no," or one of its many variations. They invited two-year-olds and their mothers to spend time in a playroom. At the end of the session, each mother was asked to have her child pick up all the toys. The children were also observed at home during dinner preparation and mealtime. This period was selected on the assumption that there would be several occasions on which the parents would need to direct and control the children.

The observations highlighted the difference between self-assertion and defiance. Having allowed the children only forty minutes to play with the multitude of appealing toys, it was guaranteed that putting them away was the farthest thing from their minds. "No, want to play" would be an example of the type of self-assertion made by the children. The way in which the mothers subsequently responded had considerable influence on whether or not the child complied or became defiant.

We all know what compliance entails; the distinction between self-assertion and defiance, however, warrants a brief discussion. Going back to Spitz's idea that saying "no" is an important sign of growing autonomy, "No, want to play" is nothing to get concerned about. It denotes the child's ability to articulate his wishes, even though his mother may have other ideas as to what he should be doing. It becomes defiance when the motive is primarily to challenge—for example, making a point of taking more toys out of the box or heaving them across the room.

Defiance was most likely to develop when parents asserted their own power through "negative control." The researchers defined this as the use of threats, criticism, physical restraint or direction, and anger. Parents who used a democratic approach, however, were more successful in securing compliance. The combination of responsiveness and control was evident from the way in which they responded to their children. They listened to what the child said and did not consider the self-assertion as an outrageous challenge to their authority. They sympathized with the child's wish to continue playing, but explained that it was time to go. The approach also used reasoning—for example, "You made the mess, so you need to clean it up." The parents were also willing to accommodate the child's objections, but only up to a point. A common example for this age group would be the offer to pick up some of the toys provided he joins in as well. Crockenberg and Litman concluded that compliance is likely to follow when parents use "strategies that combine a clear statement of what the parent wants with an acknowledgment of the child's perspective."

Susie Lamborn at the University of West Florida has a particular interest in the relationship between parenting styles and adolescent adjustment. She and her colleagues have studied many thousands of students over a period of several years and have noted the positive effect of specific characteristics of democratic parenting such as monitoring, encouragement of achievement, and joint decision-making. One of their larger studies related parenting style to the social development, academic achievement, emotional well-being, and behavioral adjustment of over four thousand high school students. Those adolescents with democratic parents had the best scores on all the measures. Another finding was the importance of balancing parental warmth, acceptance, and involvement on the one hand, with strictness and supervision on the other. The former have a strong role in the development of self-esteem and well-being, while the latter keep teens in line.

At the far end of the age spectrum, Amy Strage and Tamara Brandt at San Jose University examined the relationship between parenting style and the "mastery-oriented" student. Such a student has confidence in her ability to succeed and is persistent in her efforts to do so. Having a positive perception of authority figures, she is also likely to see instructors as a resource to be consulted when necessary. Over two hundred university students were asked to rate aspects of their relationships with their parents. Adjustment and achievement were found to be related to key characteristics of democratic parenting—high expectations combined with a high level of support, and the encouragement of independence and autonomy. The findings also demonstrated that the impact of parenting persisted even when the students were living independently. In fact, the relationship between parenting style and the outcome measures was equally strong when comparisons were made between students living at home and those who had their own accommodation.

These three studies are only a small sample of research that has been undertaken over a half century. Taken together, they provide convincing evidence that democratic parenting has a positive impact in many areas, including the motivation to achieve at school, grades in elementary and high school, social competence, confidence and self-esteem, and career aspirations. Democratic parenting is also associated with a lower incidence of behavior problems and a greater ability to cope with stress.

An additional finding may be of interest to those who are not living in nuclear families. A large Canadian study found that parenting style was more influential than family structure. While it is true that there is a slightly higher incidence of adjustment difficulties among children in non-traditional families, this is unlikely to be the result of the structure itself; rather, it can indicate the need to pay particularly close attention to parenting style. Single parents who maintain a democratic approach can expect to be as successful as those in two-parent, nuclear families. The same applies to parents in stepfamilies, in spite of the fact that they may be coping with a lengthy and sometimes painful period of adjustment.

Styles, Consistency, and Flying by the Seat of Your Pants

A moderate challenge to the idea that consistency is a hallmark of good parenting is in order. After reviewing almost one hundred studies, George Holden and Pamela Miller at the University of Texas concluded that patterns of child-rearing were both "enduring and different." While there was evidence of consistency, parents adapted their style according to both the child they were dealing with and the specific situation. Furthermore, their style was modified over time, presumably because of the child's changing needs and abilities. Holden and Miller went on to argue that the ability to be both consistent and flexible is the basis for sensitive parenting and will help children feel respected as individuals.

The balance of consistency and flexibility is probably the main reason why the democratic style has been shown to reduce the conflict between work and home. Family life typically becomes more complicated and demanding when there is no full-time homemaker to manage the domestic front. Effective time management and a communal approach to household work and child care become critical and are more likely to be found when there is emphasis on the type of communication and negotiation that characterizes democratic parenting.

When pondering the many factors that have to be considered when developing and implementing an approach to family life, parents sometimes ask me if they will ever get the balance right. My usual reply is, "I hope not." After thirty years of being a parent, I haven't been able to get it right. Why should they? I believe that all parents have to remain open to revising the way they deal with their children. Children stubbornly insist on growing up, and our approach may have to be overhauled as their needs and abilities change and develop. I see it as healthy to assume that there is always something I can be doing a lot better. While the research provides valuable ideas and guidelines, and can help us avoid some of the pitfalls, a manual for successful parenting does not exist. I doubt that it ever will.

7 Taking Care of Our Parents: The Sandwich Generation

The headline of a recent newspaper article posed the important question: "Have we abandoned our aging parents?" The reporter suggested that the answer was "yes." He portrayed baby boomers as a thoroughly self-centered lot who would be on the phone to a retirement or nursing home if their elderly parents so much as complained of a head cold. I may be exaggerating somewhat, but the tone was distinctly critical; the central thesis was that we no longer seem willing to care for our own parents, expecting the social service or health care systems to take on responsibilities that were previously assumed by the family.

This idea is yet another one of the myths that exist about family life. The truth is that the vast majority of seniors who are no longer entirely independent do remain in the community, usually with the support and assistance of their adult children. One study found that 80 percent of the care needed was provided by family members. Furthermore, the minority who are in institutions (7 percent in a recent North American survey) are there because of chronic medical conditions that necessitate a level of specialized care that families cannot provide—advanced Alzheimer's and Parkinson's are two examples.

Our willingness to care for our parents as long as possible has helped to create the "sandwich generation"—those adults who are simultaneously taking care of their children and their parents. One simple statistic illustrates the point: approximately one-third of adults with parents above the age of sixty-five will be at least partly responsible for their care.

In order to understand the challenges facing the sandwich generation, it can be helpful to discuss several trends. The first is the steady increase in life expectancy over the last century. Improvements in health care and lifestyle mean that women can expect to live into their early eighties and men into their mid-seventies. While we hope that longevity will offer us an extended and happy retirement, it also entails the risk of a gradual loss of health and independence; there is more time to develop those health and related problems that make it hard to remain independent.

Another trend is the common decision to have children later in life. The average age at marriage has increased from the early to the late twenties since the 1960s. As a result, couples may spend several years concentrating on their careers or enjoying time together before contemplating child-rearing. This means that they are more likely to be in the midst of raising their own children when their parents are becoming elderly. Given the trends in employment, it's also likely that potential caregivers will be employed. Coping with the responsibility of caring for elders thus becomes far more challenging than it was when many families had a full-time homemaker.

Preparing Ourselves

Given the inevitability of the situation, it seems odd that we pay so little attention to how we might prepare ourselves for changes in our family lives. We often seem to wait until problems arise. I believe there is, therefore, a place for the equivalent of a short course in preparation for becoming a full-fledged member of the sandwich generation. Jo Ann Lee at the University of North Carolina surveyed employees in a variety of settings who were caring for elders. Many talked about the lack of available information. The majority indicated that they would welcome resources such as support groups, seminars, and informational tapes.

Those entering the sandwich generation will find themselves in unfamiliar territory. What follows is not intended to be the definitive guidebook or road map. Rather, it is an attempt to offer ideas and suggestions that may make it easier to cope with the demands of caring for those who once cared for us.

Understanding Aging

I am a long-time fan of James Taylor. Sometimes it feels as if we have grown older together; over the years, several of his songs have seemed so relevant to my particular stage of life at the time. While the effects of aging have not yet become a major issue in my life, I nonetheless find myself drawn to the lyrics of his song, *The Secret of Life*. I particularly like the line, "Nobody knows how we got to the top of the hill, but since we're on our way down, we might as well enjoy the ride." This philosophy has become one of my major goals. Taylor's lyrics emphasize that aging can have desirable consequences and, although there are always individual differences, the general trend is for people to become more content with themselves as they get older. They are often financially secure and can enjoy the benefits of greater disposable income. While some may regret leaving the workforce, most do not. Recent data from the extensive Cornell Retirement and Well-Being Study, for example, indicated that approximately three-quarters of the people surveyed were very satisfied with retirement, and the majority found it to be an improvement over their working lives. Age also allows an accumulation of knowledge and experience. Although you should not expect people to flock around in the hope of catching one of your many pearls, you can achieve a more insightful and balanced view of the world.

At the same time, I do not believe James Taylor would have written the song if he had not been aware of how challenging it can become to enjoy the ride down. For one thing, the image of aging is not particularly favorable in our culture at this point in history. I grew up in the era when nobody over thirty was trusted; as an adolescent and young adult, I recall being absolutely convinced that the vast majority of my parents' generation simply did not "get it" and should be seen as one of society's greatest liabilities. This generation gap may be far narrower in today's world, but we are not listed among the nations known for treating older people with deference and respect. The roles given to older people in books, movies, and television shows, for example, are often less than flattering. While the elderly may be portrayed as wise and valued members of society on some occasions, they are a shoo-in when a story calls for someone who is crotchety, confused, out-of-touch, self-absorbed, or just plain foolish. Such images hardly foster self-esteem among those who are aging.

Another obstacle to an enjoyable "ride down" is the recognition that the body often reaches a point where it is no longer user-friendly. I do not want to paint too dismal a picture, but physical deterioration is an unavoidable reality. Joints become stiff, and motor tasks that were previously performed with ease can become challenging and painful. The intestinal system can seem to be operating at half-power, and having a bowel movement can be such a major undertaking that it becomes a topic for discussion. Sleep patterns change, often for the worse, and the risk of having a chronic illness or other medical disorder increases steadily as the years pass. Of course there are some people who maintain excellent health until the end of a long life, but all will face some degree of deterioration. These physical changes can bring about profound feelings of loss. It can seem as if the body has gone from being a helpful "tool" to an impediment.

It can also be frustrating, embarrassing, or even frightening to find that one's mental efficiency is simply not what it used to be. Again, there are tremendous differences in the extent to which this is true; some seniors remain "sharp" throughout their long life. But most will eventually become aware that their intellectual abilities—and in particular their memory—are weakening. Our expectations do not help. There has been interesting research into how the perception of memory skills varies with age. A person in her twenties might forget someone's name or miss an appointment and not be overly concerned; chances are, she would see it as one of those things that happen from time to time. A person in his sixties, on the other hand, might perceive exactly the same lapses of memory as indicative of his declining mental abilities. If he has a series of such lapses, he might even begin to worry that he is experiencing early signs of something more ominous, such as Alzheimer's. This research suggests that, while there *is* likely to be a general decrease in mental efficiency, its extent can be both overestimated and misinterpreted.

All of us are, of course, aware of our mortality. But this awareness is often intellectual; we know we will eventually die, but the expanse of our future makes death seem remote. Aging brings an awareness of mortality that is far more personal and emotional. The fact that most of your life has passed can generate anxiety and fear, as well as a sense of urgency. An additional factor is that time perception changes with age. People are best at estimating how much time has elapsed around the age of thirty. Younger people overestimate time; it moves more slowly for them. With advancing age, however, time's duration is underestimated; it seems to fly by, using up a commodity that is already in short supply. A line from another song, Bonnie Raitt's *Nick of Time*, comes to mind: "Life gets mighty precious when there's less of it to waste."

There are numerous manifestations of depression among seniors. It is often "subclinical" in that it would not meet the diagnostic criteria for a depressive disorder. Rather, it consists of a chronically depressed mood; much of the joy has gone out of life, and being unhappy and discontent can become the norm. This type of depression increases the risk of physical illness that, in turn, adds to the feelings of unhappiness. The relationship between emotional and physical health becomes even more pronounced when a full-blown depressive disorder is present; this factor is known to impede recovery from a number of medical conditions.

The cognitive problems associated with aging can also be intensified by higher levels of depression. Problem-solving and verbal reasoning skills can be affected adversely. One study discovered an impact on vocabulary; although the fund of words was still present, access was no longer "fluid." Knowing what you want to say and not being able to say it can be very frustrating. Such effects have been noted for both genders, although there is some evidence that men may be more susceptible.

Perhaps one of the most concerning aspects of aging is the prospect of losing independence. It is important to remember just how long our parents have been capable, independent members of society. Most will have managed jobs and careers, as well as headed their families. It would be the rare person who would ever *seek* to become dependent on others; dependency can lower self-esteem and create a situation in which one's choices become limited. After all, if you cannot perform a task yourself, when and how it will be carried out becomes a decision others will influence, if not make for you.

One of the exercises I use in groups and workshops is to ask people to share their own fears about aging. What do they least want to happen to themselves as they get older? This may sound somewhat depressing, and I have to admit that it ignores the fact that life can remain enjoyable and fulfilling no matter how old you are. But we are obviously fooling ourselves if we assume this is guaranteed. Recognizing our own fears can help us appreciate the way our parents may be feeling. Understandably, many of the responses center on illness and loss of independence. Being incontinent and not being able to feed oneself are also common items. Topping my list is Alzheimer's and the prospect of losing my mental abilities to the point where I could become verbally abusive to my children; I do not want my last words to them to be hurtful, even though they would probably understand that my disease was to blame.

The Job Description and Division of Labor

An almost obvious, but often neglected, part of preparing to care for our parents is to find out what they need from us. These are among the most common items:

1. Help with everyday activities in the community—for example, shopping, banking, or getting to medical appointments.
2. Assistance with taking medication. The number of drugs being prescribed, their side effects, and a decline in memory skills can combine to make it very hard for some seniors to keep track of what they should take and when. The risk of an accidental overdose or failure to follow through with much-needed treatment can become a perennial worry.
3. Assistance with everyday chores in the home, such as cleaning and meal preparation.
4. Assistance with specific tasks in the home such as maintenance and repair.
5. Emotional support, including regular contact just to keep in touch and combat loneliness and isolation. Not surprisingly, one study found this to be the most common item on the list of things that our aging parents will need. It is also an extension of the social support discussion found in Chapter 5. Studies show that the social isolation and loss of a support network that can accompany aging can undermine physical health among seniors.
6. Assistance with personal affairs, including being present when financial or legal arrangements are being made and offering suggestions and advice. Another common need is help in obtaining health care—for example, being part of discussions with doctors. It is not uncommon for seniors to have several complaints or disorders, each of which requires its own treatment regimen.
7. Undertaking tasks on their behalf. While we may sometimes assist our parents, there can be times when they need us to take over completely—for example, making arrangements with

tradespeople, handling financial matters on an informal basis, or exercising a fairly broad control through power of attorney.

8. Teaching skills. This item can apply to all the areas listed above. There may be situations in which our parents would prefer to maintain their independence rather than become reliant on us. One example relates to the likelihood that the husband will be the first to die or become infirm. If the marriage has been more traditional in style, the wife may not be familiar with the financial side of family life; paying bills and managing bank accounts may never have been on her list of responsibilities. Household maintenance—especially tasks requiring basic electrical or mechanical skills—can seem especially daunting, even though she is more than capable of handling them. Learning to do so can be a relief, as well as a boost to self-esteem.

Once you know what your parents need, the next step is to establish an action plan. The potential for family friction looms. While there may be families that decide matters smoothly, there are others in which resentment proves to be chronic and damaging. This can be the case when one person feels compelled to take the major responsibility while other family members are content to sit back and offer only the occasional piece of unwelcome advice or ill-founded criticism.

Division of labor is called for whenever possible. I am not suggesting that helping our elderly parents is simply a "chore." It's more a question of recognizing that people with jobs and children already have very busy and full lives, and their time is a commodity that is used up much too quickly. Sharing the responsibility makes the situation more manageable; it also reflects the idea that families, rather than individuals, care for their own.

I recommend being quite specific. Just securing a commitment that a family member will help may not actually lead to any action. It can be much more productive to have a family meeting in which each person is given a list of what needs to be done, and responsibilities are assigned. Alternatively, if one person has already become the main source of assistance and support, she could contact the others and request that they take over a specific role or task. The rhetorical question and complaint, "Why is it always me?" sometimes warrants the simple answer "Because I always say yes." Give others the opportunity to say the same.

Gender issues may need to be openly and frankly discussed. A burdened member of the family is far more likely to be a daughter or daughter-in-law than their male counterparts, once again illustrating the influence of traditional gender roles. One survey found that three-quarters of caregivers are women. In addition, women tend to feel compelled to adjust their working lives to accommodate the needs of elderly parents and are more willing to cut back their hours of employment if necessary.

Responsibility cannot always be shared equally. Geography, for example, may dictate that one sibling is more readily available than another. Kathy's parents, for example, have the benefit of a daughter who lives close to their home. In spite of her own very busy schedule, Patti visits them regularly and manages most of their affairs through power of attorney. As is the case for almost 50 percent of adult children who have elderly parents, Kathy and I live more than fifty miles away. Every so often, however, Patti calls with a specific request, often involving a medical appointment or other excursion into the community.

The family conference should be one of many. The demands of caring for parents typically multiply as their health declines. Placement in a staffed facility may eventually be needed and will decrease the demands on the family. In the meantime, however, the amount of assistance required often increases steadily. As many shoulders as possible are needed to share the load and, while caregivers are usually daughters and sons or their spouses, it may be wise to involve the youngest generation as well. The fastest-growing segment of the population is those eighty-five years or older. One consequence is that the proportion of caregivers over the age of sixty has increased; approximately 20 percent are now seventy themselves. An infusion of younger blood can only help.

Keeping a File on Your Parents

Sometimes being a psychologist is a distinct liability. Several years ago Kathy and her siblings decided that it was high time they found out more about their parents' affairs. One particularly difficult issue was to determine their wishes regarding their funerals. I was voted the person most qualified to conduct the interview. The fact that my training and experience in psychology offered absolutely no preparation for this task was of no concern to them, but in reflection perhaps I was not such a bad choice. I had a close enough relationship with them to feel I had license to raise such a topic. At the same time, I was distant enough that I did not find the discussion too emotionally distressing.

My most lasting impression is that neither of my in-laws seemed upset that I had broached the subject of their mortality; on the contrary, both seemed very happy, if not relieved, to be able to communicate their wishes. It was also evident that my mother-in-law, in particular, had thought about such matters at length. She had no difficulty listing the fine details—she knew the music she wanted played at the funeral mass, the type of dress she wanted to wear, and who could be trusted to choose it.

In typical fashion, my father-in-law feigned indifference. After listening to his wife's detailed instructions, he assured me that all the family had to do was bury him in the back garden. When I pointed out that I was sure municipal bylaws prohibited this practice and added that the best we could hope for between November and March was storage in a snowbank, he became more realistic.

I was surprised at how much information we did not have. My in-laws had already paid for their grave sites, and they provided details as to where the necessary paperwork could be found. I learned about their insurance policies, the location of their wills, and the person they wanted to have power of attorney if one was needed. They also sought my opinion about the executors of their will and explained their wishes about what should happen if they became incapable of living independently. There have certainly been much easier conversations, but this one did not prove overly difficult. Once I overcame my initial reservations, it was not hard to continue.

Redefining Family Relationships

It is important to bear in mind that our relationships with our aging parents will be very different from those that existed during our childhoods. This change has been described as a progression from "engagement" to "disengagement," and then to "re-engagement." Initial engagement is the process of developing the attachment to our parents that begins the moment we are born. As we enter adolescence and approach adulthood, however, we need to separate to the point where we have the confidence and skills required to become independent adults. Such disengagement does not have to mean loss of close emotional ties; it simply refers to the likelihood that we are no longer dependent on our parents and the fact that we will have self-sufficient lifestyles as adults, just as they will as empty-nesters. Re-engagement is the stage when our relationship with our parents becomes very involved again; this time, however, it is because of *their* dependency rather than ours. In this respect, it is a very different relationship. Our new role is far removed from that of the child we once were. While our childhood roles are no longer viable, it is very easy for adult children and their parents to slip back into old patterns. Doing so can create a great deal of tension and dissatisfaction.

Although the process of re-engagement is typically discussed in the context of parent-child relationships, it can also be applied to siblings. While brothers and sisters may maintain contact with one another, they almost always lead independent lives. The sibling relationship may exist only to meet emotional and social needs. Such a purpose is, of course, both important and sufficient; however, not having to work together avoids resurrecting rivalries that existed when we were fighting over who had the most chores and the fewest privileges. Working together as adults requires the same process of re-engagement; this can become problematic when the past seems more influential than the present.

I am reminded of how enduring these old patterns can be whenever I participate in family reunions. Most I attend involve members of Kathy's family. I hasten to add that I have not been disowned by my own; they just happen to live more than four thousand miles away. Observing Kathy and her family together never ceases to impress upon me how quickly people can revert to their past scripts. The five siblings are fully grown, independent, mature, and responsible adults who are very involved in their working and parenting roles. But at least part of each reunion is devoted to reasserting the old power structure and re-enacting the sibling rivalries that have been unresolved for more than thirty years. My younger brother-in-law has no intention of ever totally forgiving his three older sisters for collectively deciding that oppression and domination were the best tools for building his character. My older brother-in-law, who recalls changing his younger siblings' diapers, still likes to point out when he feels they are making messes and offer advice as to how they should be cleaned up. While the rivalry is almost always good-natured and is often staged for its entertainment value, it is nonetheless real.

With the goals of preparation and prevention in mind, I would like to discuss some ideas about re-engaging with our parents in a way that can be both satisfying and successful.

Becoming Assertive—I'm a Grown-Up, Too!

You would think that after being an independent person for decades, your parents would finally get the hint that you have grown up. Sometimes this does not seem to be the case. One reason can be that their most fondly remembered involvement in your life occurred when you were anything but grown up. They fed you, changed you, and otherwise ran most aspects of your life. Moreover, although they may have plenty of examples of how wonderful you were back then, they probably have a store of other memories to illustrate just how irresponsible you could be at times.

Sometimes, I find myself struggling to recognize that two of our children are well into adulthood; it has been over ten years since the younger one left home. That did not deter me, however, from asking him at least seven times if he had his passport and ticket when we headed off to England for a visit. Being a good-natured fellow, Tim bit his tongue and did not remind me that he has traveled far more in his life than I have in mine. During the course of the trip, we visited my mother in a chronic care nursing home. After leaving, Tim informed me that I would always have a home with him if I could no longer care for myself. While never doubting his sincerity, it took me a while to find this reassuring. After all, if he were to take care of me in the same way he once cared for his goldfish, I was doomed.

There is no adequate substitute for open communication when issues relating to re-engagement become troublesome. A common complaint voiced in groups and workshops is that while parents want assistance, they treat their adult children as if they were less than competent when it comes to providing it. Not addressing this matter creates a fertile ground for resentment and frustration. Often grown-up children are too understanding: they know how hard it must be for their parents to admit they need help and are willing to put up with the criticism and lack of appreciation.

I like to draw on the experiences I had with assertiveness-training groups when I was a student. We had a lot of fun and emerged as experts at returning defective goods and expressing our complaints to people without resorting to primitive forms of violence or becoming overwhelmed by guilt. We included a lot of role-playing and utilized a three-step model of assertiveness:

Assertiveness Training 101
Step 1: Communicating empathy
Empathy is a critical component involving both acknowledgment of how the other person may be feeling and understanding of their position and opinion. Without empathy, people can emerge

feeling that they have treated the other person unfairly. Communicating empathy becomes especially important when we need to be assertive with our parents. There can be many reasons why we are reluctant to say things that could upset them.

Step 2: Communicating your views and feelings
You would not, of course, have any need to assert yourself if you agreed with the other person's take on the matter. It is important, therefore, to make sure that the other person understands how *you* think and feel. Every once in a while this aspect of assertiveness may prove to be futile. There is always a risk that it will be met with a look of complete disdain and indifference, but I would expect most family members to be more receptive. You might end up being pleasantly surprised at hearing a version of "I never knew you felt this way," or "I wish you had told me sooner."

Step 3: Requesting what you want
Unfortunately, people often skip this last step, failing to make any suggestions about improving the situation. What is clearly needed is a solution that will make everyone happy. If happiness is not in the cards, you can always settle for a solution that at least lessens the misery and feels fair.

Omission of this step is most likely to occur when the first step has been missed as well. This downgrades the communication from assertiveness to whining. If the emotion is strong enough, the whole effort can achieve the status of a tirade. Pent-up resentment is unleashed with a force that stuns the recipient, and your only accomplishment is to make yourself feel guilty.

An example can always help. A woman in one of our groups was becoming more and more resentful of the fact that her parents never seemed to appreciate what she did for them. It could be something as small as doing the dishes when she was over, although on other occasions more time-consuming tasks were involved. She began to feel as if her parents took her for granted or believed that she "owed" them. What was even more upsetting was the fact that any comments her parents did make tended to be negative—they frequently found reasons to criticize her, even when she had gone out of her way to be helpful.

I cannot recall a single role-play in which the other group members did not come up with a wide variety of "scripts." I have never recorded any of them, but the following would be fairly close to the script she decided was best for her:

"I know how hard it must be for you to depend on other people for so much, and I know you are both feeling tired and unwell a lot of the time (Step 1). But as much as I am happy to help out whenever I can, it upsets me that you never show any appreciation. If I hear anything, it is usually a criticism or complaint (Step 2). I would like it so much if you would please let me know that what I do is helpful and appreciated (Step 3)."

It can sometimes seem contrived to dissect assertiveness in this way. I am convinced, however, that many people live with a great deal of unnecessary hurt and frustration because they are unable to find ways to express themselves or ask for change. I was raised in a family where we were told repeatedly, "If you haven't anything nice to say, don't say anything." While the comments my brother and I made to one another rarely embodied this principle, I grew up feeling that self-assertion was in the same ballpark as complaining and verbal aggression. It took a while for me to learn that assertion is an important part of protecting and strengthening relationships. Thinking in terms of the three steps was a useful way of ensuring that I communicated everything I wanted to express.

Re-engaging with parents and siblings involves much revision and negotiation of roles. Communication and assertiveness increase the likelihood that this renewed involvement will be based on mutual understanding and respect, and will constitute a partnership of equals.

Accepting the Past

As much as people strive for harmony, old patterns of behavior can be really tough to change. One of the participants in the group I just mentioned talked about the unlikelihood that the script would work for her. Her childhood had not been very happy, and she had long since abandoned any hope that she could ever gain her parents' approval. They had not been close, and contact became infrequent after she left home. She nonetheless felt an obligation to assist them now that they were having difficulty caring for themselves. Her approach was to combine acceptance and humor. She reminded us of the saying, "God grant me the serenity to accept the things I cannot change, the courage to change the things I can, and the wisdom to know the difference." The humor aspect of her approach was illustrated by an account of her last visit home. Her parents always accused her of being neglectful; no matter how recently she had been there, she could count on being greeted with, "About time! Why don't you ever come to see us?" Similarly, her departure always prompted, "You're going so soon?" She relayed how she had started off the conversation on her most recent visit. It began something like, "I know, I know. It's been so long you probably don't even recognize who I am..."

Such an approach may not suit everyone. Sometimes people opt for silence. Our relationships with our parents when we were children may have been good, but they were never perfect. Living with the people you love is as much about tolerating what we see as their faults as it is about enjoying their positive attributes. When assertiveness and humor fail, a stoic acceptance interspersed with occasional venting is perhaps the best course of action.

Taking Care of Yourself

It is important to emphasize that the majority of people who are caring for their parents reach a point where they feel able to manage the added responsibilities quite well. Some writers have commented on the myth of the suffering sandwich generation, criticizing others who refer to "intergenerational caregiving" as a burden that threatens the well-being of the family. As has been discussed several times, changes in family life often lead to doom-and-gloom predictions that prove unfounded. This also applies to the sandwich generation. For example, studies have shown that the quality of a marriage is unrelated to the extent to which one spouse is involved in elder care. While estimates vary, it also seems that approximately two-thirds of people in the sandwich generation do *not* find that caring for their parents has a profoundly negative impact on their work or family lives.

The need to take care of ourselves nonetheless remains. Presumably, the more that is done in this department, the greater the likelihood that we will not be among the one-third who *are* finding it hard to deal with the demands on their time and energy. Those in this sizable minority often doubt their ability to care for their parents without some type of support. They may also be contemplating reducing their hours of employment or quitting work altogether, and their level of job satisfaction tends to diminish.

Just as it is hard for a parent to ensure that all child care activities take place outside normal working hours, maintaining the separation between work and elder care can be difficult. Having to take a parent to a medical appointment can require time off during normal working hours; distance, availability of appointments, and the punctuality of doctors rarely allow the task to be accomplished in a lunch break. Gail Hepburn and Julian Barling at Queen's University in Ontario conducted a detailed study of the impact of elder care responsibilities on the day-to-day working lives of women and men. On average, participants had been caring for parents for almost ten years. "Partial absences" directly related to elder care responsibilities were frequent and included telephone calls, arriving late and having to leave early, extended break times, and being distracted to the point where they were no longer concentrating on their job.

Stress levels may rise steadily. Studies have found that those caring for parents suffering from Alzheimer's, for example, experience three times the number of symptoms associated with stress than others in their age range. They are also likely to find that their performance at work diminishes while their number of sick days increases.

Approaches to self-care and time management have already been discussed; the action plan and division of labor referred to earlier in this chapter are also part and parcel of making sure we look out for ourselves as well as our parents. But I would like to discuss one more area—this relates to the complex emotions we can experience when faced with the reality of caring for our parents. It is an entirely different experience than caring for our children. Raising children almost always takes place in an atmosphere of optimism and hope. We watch them grow and applaud their achievements. The hard times and rough periods rarely go on for ever. Watching our parents deteriorate, we cannot help but be aware of how much they have lost. Time is not on their side, and the prospect that their decline will be halted only by death is depressing to say the least. The future often seems both uncertain and bleak.

A few years ago, I was asked to conduct a small group session at a corporate conference. The participants were women dealing with the challenges of caring for their elderly and dependent parents. The small size of the group permitted a level of sharing and intensity that I had not encountered in previous workshops on the same topic. It soon became quite an emotional and moving experience for all of us. People talked about how distressing it could be to see their parents lose their abilities, independence, and enthusiasm for life. The perception of loss was heightened by the participants' memories. If you meet an elderly person for the first time, it may not be at all difficult to accept them for who they are now. It can also be hard to imagine them in their younger days. Our strongest images of our parents, however, are often held over from childhood. In these happier days, our parents were fit, active, and, for the most part, admired because of their ability to provide for our material and emotional needs. While love and respect can remain, the memories of the past make us painfully aware of their loss, as well as our own.

As the session grew more intense, one group member began talking about how angry and frustrated she became when her parents made it hard to help them. They were often critical of her efforts and would complain to other family members who, in turn, would imply that she was not doing a good job. She spoke in an almost apologetic tone and seemed reassured when she discovered she was not the only person who felt this way. Another shared experience was the guilt that went along with feeling angry; empathy for our parents can make it hard to accept that we still have the right to feel upset when they do not treat us fairly. Feelings of inadequacy were also expressed. One woman talked about the frequent need to make a three-hour round trip to help her mother deal with a recurrent household maintenance problem. As much as she tried to fix the problem and show her mother how she might avoid its recurrence, she could guarantee an urgent phone call within a few weeks.

The opportunity to express and discuss the emotional impact of caring for parents may not change the realities of the day-to-day demands on our lives, but it has been shown to have a "trickle-down" effect. One study looked at the benefits of attending a support group. Participants found the group helpful in a number of ways; their spouses and children also reported that family life had improved, presumably because of the general reduction in stress.

I feel almost obligated to end this chapter on an upbeat note. In trying to understand why, I was reminded of the difficulty our culture has in dealing with death and dying. We have grown up watching sitcoms that idealize family life. Problems are solved by the third commercial break, and happiness is restored before the credits roll. The increase in life expectancy over recent decades, however, has inevitably forced us to confront the realities of dying. Of course, a long, happy, and active life that ends abruptly in death is possible and, for many of us, preferred over the alternatives. But we cannot avoid the possibility that death will be preceded by a period of deterioration, ill health, and loss of independence. So, perhaps I should close with a realistic rather than a happy ending. As members of the sandwich generation, we are becoming steadily better at learning how to meet the needs of our parents, while also caring for our families. Assuming a role in caring for our parents can nonetheless be difficult, frustrating, demanding, and depressing. But it also allows us to feel that we have accomplished one of the most important goals for family life—to support, nurture, and protect one another to the best of our ability.

# 8

Help on the Horizon: Family-Friendly Employment

As students of human behavior, psychologists are often asked to make predictions. Over the years, I have learned that the best answer to questions about the way things will be in the future is "maybe" or "I haven't got a clue." Such an approach does not do much for repeat business, but it is ethical; predicting behavior is very difficult, and I don't like being wrong. With my attitude, I definitely would not make a good futurist. Such folk put themselves on the line and, in the case of working world predictions for the new millennium, have often proved themselves very wrong.

The growth of technology towards the end of the last century prompted the futurists to predict a looming crisis. We were assured that robots, computers, and other such devices would render vast sectors of the workforce redundant. If we had a job, it would likely require many less hours than we were accustomed to working. The looming crisis had to do with all the extra time we'd have on our hands. How would we fill it? The futurists saw an urgent need for us to revamp our lives, filling them with stimulating and worthwhile leisure pursuits. If we did not, we were destined to live out the rest of our days in a meaningless, vegetative state.

I can remember finding such predictions very credible. During my early working life, I saw the definition of "full-time" fall in terms of the number of hours of work. But the futurists showed the same powers of prediction as economists and meteorologists—and psychologists. Exactly the opposite happened. On average, the work week in North America has increased by more than three hours since 1970 and most of us would just love to have a chance to face the "challenge" of coping with too much time on our hands.

Had the futurists been right, there would almost certainly be less conflict between work and home. Balancing the two obviously becomes much easier when the amount of time devoted to employment decreases. The absence of such a trend, however, requires that other approaches be used to make it easier for people to accommodate the demands of work and home.

Just Do Your Job

Let's be honest: there were ways in which traditional gender roles made life simpler. Most employees were male. They did not have to concern themselves with day-to-day family issues and were free to focus exclusively on being an employee. The fact that the employee might also be the father of a young child or the son of an ailing parent was of little relevance. He was expected to keep his homelife at home and get on with his job.

I am not trying to paint a picture of heartless employers who viewed Ebenezer Scrooge as their role model, but the separation of the genders meant there was little need to even consider "family-friendly" policies or programs to help employees balance work and home. When we were growing up, my father's boss was always thought of as a kindly old gentleman. From my perspective, his practice of giving us a box of candy bars every Christmas was more than sufficient to bestow this title on him. Apart from this, nothing he did had any direct relevance to our family.

There are still employers who expect their workers to maintain this type of separation between work and home. Although I am an advocate for family-friendly work environments, I am not without sympathy for the employers' viewpoint. After all, employers are paying someone to do a job; the contract is straightforward—labor in return for money. If the employer has a philanthropic nature and strives to accommodate his employees' family lives through provision of day care, implementation of flex-time, or giving out candy at Christmas, it is a bonus rather than a right.

The debate about the ethical or social obligations of employers may, in the long run, be of little practical significance. Writers in the field have argued that change in the direction of family-friendly work policies is likely to be driven more by good economic sense. Retaining employees has become a problem in many fields. With the birth rate in decline, and the baby boom generation getting ready to call it quits, a shortage of skilled workers is expected. A recent newspaper article noted that "As boomers retire, employers find they're fishing for talent in a puddle instead of a pool."

The economic incentive to keep skilled staff is substantial. Companies can expect to pay up to one-and-a-half times an employee's annual salary to find and train a replacement. Recognizing that men are more involved in family life than before, and acknowledging that a sizable segment of the labor force consists of women in their child-rearing years, policies designed to reduce the conflict between work and home can give employers a competitive edge when it comes to attracting and retaining workers.

The prospect of reducing absenteeism is an additional incentive. A Conference Board of Canada survey of four hundred organizations in 1992 showed that absenteeism had risen by 30 percent over the previous three years. Comparable statistics have emerged from studies in the United States and other industrialized nations. A major factor contributing to this rise in absenteeism is the increased presence of women with preschool children who are finding it hard to balance work and home. Needing time off to take care of aging and ill parents is also a factor. The view that work-family conflict has led to a rise in absenteeism received support from Linda Duxbury at Carleton University in Ottawa. She compared absenteeism rates of workers reporting high or low levels of work-family conflict. Significant differences were found among workers in clerical, administrative, retail, and production positions. On average, those in the high-conflict group were absent eight days per year, as compared to three days for the low-conflict group.

The proponents for family-friendly work environments cite other benefits. In general, the expectation is that workers will be more satisfied and less stressed, which, in turn, will increase productivity.

Redesigning Work

Given the potential benefits, it's not surprising that discussions of "redesigning" work are becoming popular. A recent article in *Maclean's* discussed the importance of employers recognizing that active and creative steps are needed in order to make the workplace more family-friendly. The author, Patricia Chisholm, mentioned a number of prominent companies that have taken the lead in offering employees a wide range of benefits and services in order to accommodate the demands of their family lives. I cannot hope to cover all of the ideas that have been put forward, but I would like to discuss some of the more popular.

Telecommuting

Telecommuting, or "telework," is based on the premise that technology can transform the home into a "virtual office." The most common tools are the telephone, fax machine, and computer with Internet access. Many of the tasks that might previously have been carried out in an office can now be completed at home. Large amounts of material and information can be communicated between the worker and either the employer or client with a few simple clicks of the mouse.

At first glance, telecommuting can be reminiscent of that period in history when work and home were combined. But there are important differences. Perhaps the most important is the fact that the worker is still very much part of an outside organization.

Regardless of the amount of time he is at home, he must remain an active member of the organization.

The opportunity for employees to be home-based has appeal as a way of balancing the demands of work and family. It would be hard, however, to find another area of occupational research that has yielded such varied results. Telecommuting can prove to be a rip-roaring success for all concerned, but it can also have the opposite outcome. If the current trend continues, up to 20 percent of the North American workforce will be at least partially telecommuting by 2010. The benefits and costs of this type of arrangement are, therefore, important to examine.

Employees who like telecommuting talk about its flexibility. Getting their children to the dentist or their elderly parents to a lawyer's appointment becomes much easier in their schedules. Telecommuting provides an opportunity for employees to be with their children, and it can reduce or eliminate the need for day care. Enthusiastic telecommuters talk about the advantages with respect to leisure activities. They can play tennis or take a quiet stroll in the mid-afternoon, knowing that they can complete their day's work later on.

Decreased living costs are another benefit. In addition to the reduced need for day care, employees do not have to travel to work or buy lunch at the cafeteria. The budget for clothing can also be cut. The cover of *Maclean's* shows someone who has taken this to an extreme. While many of us might not want to follow her lead of working in the nude (I hasten to add that her open laptop acts as a modesty shield), putting on jeans and a t-shirt first thing in the morning is a much better start to the day than having to decide how to dress for success.

There can also be a number of benefits for employers. They need less space for employees to work, as well as less space for washrooms, staff rooms, and cafeterias. Furthermore, some studies have found that productivity increases, as does employee commitment to the organization. This latter factor decreases turnover.

Unfortunately, not all of the reviews are favorable. Although employees can find it difficult when they are expected to keep their personal lives out of the workplace, they can encounter problems when the two are mixed. Studies in this area talk about the importance of "boundaries"—the simple principle that there is a time and a place for everything. Boundaries help us organize and structure our lives. Going to work typically means entering a very different type of environment than a home. Everything around you is a reminder of why you are there. The recliner, channel changer, and refrigerator have been replaced by an office chair, work bench, and computer. There is no children's artwork pinned on the bulletin board, and you do not have to worry about tripping over toys. People wear clothes that are often reserved for work, and the decor is very different from that in the average family room. All of these environmental stimuli and cues provide the boundaries that separate work from home and remind you of what you are supposed to be doing in order to get paid.

It is not uncommon to hear people complain about the amount of time they spend commuting. One of its few saving graces, however, is that the commute contributes to the positive impact of boundaries. Work is physically left behind. People can read newspapers, tune into their favorite radio station, or just stare out of the window with vacant expressions—without fear of being reprimanded.

I can speak directly to the issue of what can happen when you are confronted with a lack of boundaries. Technology allows me to work at home whenever I write, prepare reports, or consult to agencies in other communities. At this very moment, Alexandra is inquiring about the availability of Popsicles. This is a pressing issue in her life, next to which my need to meet my publisher's deadline is insignificant. I concede that addressing the Popsicles issue will not require extensive discussion or problem-solving, but it is one of a list of distractions guaranteeing that this chapter will not be finished today. The cat is upgrading his whine to a howl—probably also in complaint about the lack of nourishment—and I have had to make two trips to collect children from school. I also made many more trips to the kitchen in keeping with my behavior modification program. This entitles me to a snack after completing a page of the manuscript and accounts for the fact that I put on a good fifteen pounds every time I write a book. My dentist's office phoned to suggest that, provided I still had some remaining teeth, arranging a long-overdue checkup would not be such a bad idea. I also had to field a call (probably from another telecommuter) about buying a magazine subscription. Actually, it has not been such a bad day. Trying to work at home on weekends is an even more formidable task. There's far too much going on, and I even suffer the odd pang of guilt over not doing my fair share of the domestic chores.

The boundary issue also relates to physical space. Research indicates that boundaries are much clearer when the worker has a separate office area in the home, ideally out of bounds to other people. With five of us in the home all needing use of a computer, I do not have the luxury of my own designated space. It may be rationalization on my part, but I like to think that I also would not *want* to have an area of the house that is inaccessible to the children. Others in my position also talk about their wish to remain approachable; young children, in particular, cannot be expected to appreciate that a parent is at work when he is at home. So our children wander in, the keyboard gets stickier and stickier, and dishes are left on the desk just as they are everywhere else in the house. I am also convinced that the kids have set up a small business selling all my pens, erasers, and staplers to their friends.

Boundaries can also be set in terms of time. When you go to work, you have a definite start and end time; to varying degrees, telecommuters set their own hours. You might think that this encourages them to work less. In fact, they tend to do exactly the opposite. Telecommuters often do not seem to know when to stop and give their employers more than their money's worth.

Staying in touch electronically can be beneficial, but not always. The term "electronic leash" has been used to refer to the Big Brother element of always being accessible. I remember sitting next to an employee of an international bank on a flight across Canada. He lamented that, as much as he was putting geographical distance between himself and his office in Europe, he might as well be back at his desk. Although he was grateful that airlines forbade the use of cell phones during flight, he was expected to be one of those people you see walking into the terminal already immersed in conversation or retrieving voice mail. As much as he enjoyed the comfort of flying business class, he knew his company was not spending the money out of concern for his welfare. Like the other travelers who grab a quick cup of coffee before finding a booth in the business class lounge, he would be plugging in his laptop to answer his voluminous e-mail.

Electronic mail and the telephone may facilitate communication in certain ways, but they limit it in others. Nonverbal cues such as facial expressions and body posture, for example, tell us a lot about how people are feeling and what they are truly thinking. As a result, the absence of face-to-face contact can be an obstacle to effective communication with supervisors and other employees.

Telecommuters may operate on a set work day, but those who do not can find themselves open for business at all hours. The electronic leash can result in feeling always "on call" and may become a source of resentment and pressure that adds to the work-family conflict.

Another challenge for companies introducing telecommuting is to ensure adequate training and supervision for their employees. You do not have the day-to-day contact with others that allows you to either learn from them or be accountable to your boss. Similarly, you are not readily able to pass on your skills and expertise to others. Working as a team is not impossible; teleconferencing, for example, can make it easy to have contact with even a wider range of people than would be possible in a traditional office. At the same time, however, the day-to-day interactions—scheduled and unscheduled—that occur in many workplaces are no longer feasible. In addition to the impact on management and training, the lack of personal contact can reduce the degree of emotional support that people derive from relationships at work. This isolation can have negative effects that spill over into home life. It can also present problems for certain employees; those prone to depression or alcohol abuse, for example, may find that the lack of social contact and structure adds to their difficulties.

There will inevitably be jobs that do not lend themselves to telecommuting. Many occupations in the industrial sector, for example, require people to be on-site. In situations where telecommuting is possible, however, its prevalence is on the rise. The research into the impact of telecommuting is also expanding and should, over time, help employers and employees determine when it can reduce the conflict between work and home and when it should be avoided. Currently, there is not a great deal of information to guide this decision, although one predictor of success is the extent to which the employee already possesses good time-management skills. Gender may also be a factor. There are some indications that telecommuting is harder for women to implement, primarily because they are the ones expected to answer the call whenever domestic issues requiring a parent arises. Given the trend towards greater equity in distribution of family tasks, this gender difference may gradually disappear. A final factor that has been shown to predict success is the extent to which the telecommuter has a supportive supervisor. Although this relationship may be primarily through cyberspace or telephone calls, it provides a critical link to the organization and can provide the encouragement, feedback, and assistance that most employees value.

Part-Time Employment

There is a distinctly arbitrary quality to the definition of full-time work. Some studies consider more than thirty hours a week to be full-time; none of my employers ever did. They held the view that you should demonstrate your commitment to the job by acting as if going home before the witching hour was a rare treat.

One argument for abandoning arbitrary notions of full- and part-time employment is to help effect a change of attitude. When people make assumptions about who is likely to be more committed to the job, the full-time employee is usually given the vote of confidence. Such an assumption, however, is more of a stereotype than a true reflection of the working world. Thinking back to my days as a part-time faculty member at a university, I worked alongside a number of professors who were, in principle, full-time. In reality, they had retired many years ago but had neglected to tell the rest of us. I recall a colleague who believed that at least one professor had progressed from retirement to hibernation. Although I might be biased in my perception, those of us in part-time positions were at least as dedicated to the job as the others and felt the same level of commitment to our students.

Although I could find research to support my opinion, I would need to be selective in my choice of data. Some studies find that not only are part-time employees as committed to the job as their full-time counterparts but also do the job just as well. Other findings, however, favor the full-timers. One determining factor has nothing to do directly with the worker; rather, it is the attitude and behavior of the boss. Part-time employees who feel they are treated just as well as those in full-time positions tend to be highly committed to the organization.

Although the findings are inconsistent, there is sufficient justification for concluding that part-time employees take their work seriously and do it well. This more positive attitude encourages employers to view all positions—regardless of the number of hours worked—as potential careers for those who occupy them. Being treated equally implies proportional benefits and opportunities for promotion; a frequent complaint of part-time workers is that neither exist.

Whether or not a move towards upgrading the status of part-time employment will occur remains to be seen, but the sheer number of workers involved may provide the necessary momentum. The increase in part-time positions in North America has outstripped the growth in full-time employment and now accounts for approximately 25 percent of all jobs in the labor market. One particular variation of part-time work popular among women with small children is "job-sharing," in which the employer allows a full-time position to filled by two or more workers.

Not all part-time positions are voluntary—sometimes employees are given no choice, either because of insufficient work or the employer's wish to avoid paying benefits. The opportunity to choose part-time work, however, is one way to make it easier to balance work and home; a consistent finding from comparisons of full-time and part-time employees is that the latter group report significantly less stress in their lives.

Flex-Time, Compressed Work Weeks, and Time Off

In the not too distant past, there was no negotiation when it came to the time you started work and left for home. Sometimes this rigidity is still required; when you build cars, you cannot stop the assembly line for a couple of hours because the worker who puts the wheels on doesn't clock in until eleven. But there is room for flexibility in many other workplaces. This fact has prompted a number of companies to allow employees considerable choice as to when they work. One very recent survey of more than one thousand organizations found that two-thirds offered flexible work schedules.

Early discussions of flex-time had an optimistic, positive tone—it was assumed that employees would be happier, absenteeism would go down, and productivity would go up. A "win-win" outcome of this nature has been documented—but not always. Much depends on the nature of the organization. Extra time may become necessary for management of flex-time; organizing staff can be more difficult when people have varying schedules. Flex-time can also interfere with relationships with other organizations. We typically know when we can reach the people we need to contact for work-related purposes. This predictability makes for efficiency; it can be frustrating to have to remember when different people are available. This factor could explain the findings reported by Boris Baltes and his associates at Wayne State University. They reviewed numerous studies in this area and found beneficial effects when flex-time was not too flexible. When employees had a relatively large degree of choice, however, the benefits started to decline. Problems with coordination and scheduling were seen as the likely reason.

The idea of a compressed work week provided the rationalization for my decision to make Friday a day of rest, relaxation, and preferably mindless activity. I tried not to make the change in my routine too obvious, knowing that it might evoke some negative reactions from the other members of the household, all of whom are locked into a five-day week. However, the fact that I was still unshaven as they were heading out the door and had shown no inclination of abandoning my newspaper and pot of coffee gave them a clue that something was up. They may not be convinced, but I really do compress my work week; the amount of time devoted to my practice has not declined, but it is divided over four rather than five days. I do eventually get dressed and find sufficient energy to run errands that would otherwise fill up Saturday. I will even make myself look presentable when I meet one of the children for lunch. The difference is that I can usually start the weekend in a state of relative calm rather than utter exhaustion. I am among the many fans of the compressed work week, which has gained increasing popularity, especially in the manufacturing sectors.

Day Care

Telling a parent not to worry is an exercise in futility. We are programmed to worry and we do it with passion and panache. Being at work and not feeling confident that our children are being well cared for is nothing short of torment. Employer-subsidized day care—either on-site or through block purchasing of spots in a local center—is a costly but popular solution. The presence of women in the workforce, together with their wish to return to their careers while their children are preschoolers, almost guarantees that this will be a powerful incentive to join and stay with a company. The availability of subsidized day care can be especially important for single parents, most of whom support their families on relatively low incomes.

Provision of day care has sometimes created an element of resentment among workers who either do not need this service or who are on a waiting list for a spot. The perception that the worker whose child is in day care is receiving a benefit while others are not is, of course, accurate and can lead to accusations of unfair treatment. To make matters more complicated, resentment can arise when day care is *not* available. As much as the other people at work may be sympathetic when you have child care problems, they may also be less than pleased with the effect it has on them. Almost half of the people surveyed in a large company reported that their work had been disrupted by other employees' child care problems—for example, having to cover for someone who was forced to take a day off because her babysitter was sick. On-site day care can reduce this problem, and a majority of workers express support for providing this service.

Approximately one-third of absences from work are the result of employees' needing to care for sick children. One company's creative response was to purchase spots in a day care center that accepted children who were ill. Although the spaces were not always filled, the program was deemed cost-effective because of the money saved through reduced absenteeism.

Wellness, Education, and Counseling

I recently attended a wellness fair for government employees, where participants could enjoy a massage before heading off to attend workshops or drop by the many exhibits and demonstrations. At the end of the day, they emerged with abundant information on topics such as holistic medicine, nutrition, tai chi, stress reduction, reflexology, and laser therapy. I could not help but think back to my stint as a pensions clerk in the British civil service of the early sixties. A spoon to stir our tea at break time would have made us feel nothing short of pampered—but I'm not bitter.

The fair's chief organizer was also one of the staff providing confidential counseling for employees. This is a relatively recent trend that reflects the view that an essential part of taking care of business is taking care of employees. This thinking is also proactive—for example, recognizing the early signs of the type of marital strain that can result from the conflict between work and home provides the opportunity to initiate counseling before the situation deteriorates.

Sometimes information will be sufficient to avert problems. Organizations can provide packages or seminars that inform employees of services available in the community, such as resources for elder care and registries of child care facilities. Most of the time, we are more than adept at figuring out the details for ourselves—it is just easier when someone points us in the right direction.

The Return of the Treadmill

I need to preface this section with a solemn oath that what follows is absolutely true. There has been interest in returning to the treadmill, which was a popular punishment in Victorian prisons. This time, however, it has been proposed as a benefit to the employee as opposed to a form of servitude. While I have extolled the virtues of building exercise into one's regular daily activities, the advocate of the modern-day treadmill extended this notion into the workplace. The idea is to design work stations so that otherwise sedentary employees are standing on an exercise treadmill while doing their jobs. I can live with the prospect of bank tellers drenched in sweat by mid-morning, but I hope my dentist does not decide to give it a try.

Less-ambitious programs take exercise just as seriously but opt for the more conventional gym and exercise room. The benefit is simple: exercise reduces stress, and lowered stress makes for better concentration and performance.

The Feeling of Control

There has been a move away from top-down models of control in many areas of life. The democratic parenting style discussed in Chapter 6, for example, does not give everyone equal power, but it does incorporate the view that joint decision-making is preferred over a more authoritarian approach. In the working world, there has also been a movement towards a web-like organizational structure. In this model, there is a center of power, but decision-making is a responsibility that spreads out to other parts of the web. The emphasis is on consultation and consensus, and it seems that organizations using this approach can be very effective.

One of the main reasons why family-friendly policies can lead to a reduction of stress is that they give the employee a sense of control; it is hard to balance the various aspects of your life when you have no control over them. Something as simple as a supervisor permitting personal calls when pressing family matters arise relieves the stress that can result when such calls have to be postponed or made secretively. Flex-time and the option of on-site day care also allow the parent to feel she can organize her life in a way that best meets the needs of her child as well as her employer.

Researchers Linda Thomas and Daniel Ganster developed a scale to measure the extent to which people feel they have control over areas of work and family life. They selected the areas on the basis of their known contribution to the work-family conflict. I have found the questionnaire useful during workshops where we are focusing on the application of family-friendly practices.

The Control Scale

Answer the questions on the following 5-point scale: 1, very little; 2, a little; 3, some; 4, much; 5, very much.

1. How much choice do you have over the amount and quality of day care available for your child?	1	2	3	4	5
2. How much choice do you have over the amount and quality of care available for a sick child?	1	2	3	4	5
3. How much choice do you have in obtaining adult supervision for your child/children before or after school?	1	2	3	4	5

4. How much choice do you   1   2   3   4   5
    have over the amount and
    quality of day care available
    for a dependent parent or
    other relative?

---

5. How much choice do you   1   2   3   4   5
    have over when you begin
    and end each workday or
    each workweek?

---

6. How much choice do you   1   2   3   4   5
    have in arranging part-time
    employment?

---

7. To what extent can you   1   2   3   4   5
    choose to do some of your
    work at home instead of
    your usual place of
    employment?

---

8. How much choice do you   1   2   3   4   5
    have over the amount and
    timing of work you must do
    at home in order to meet
    your employment
    demands?

---

9. How much choice do you   1   2   3   4   5
    have over the amount you
    pay for dependent care?

---

10. How much choice do you   1   2   3   4   5
    have over when you take
    vacations or days off?

11. How much control do you have over when you can take a few hours off?	1	2	3	4	5
12. To what extent are you expected to limit the number of times you make or receive personal phone calls while you work?	1	2	3	4	5
13. How much choice do you have in making unanticipated child care arrangements (e.g., during snow days or unexpected job delays)?	1	2	3	4	5
14. In general, how much control do you have over the way you balance working and parenting?	1	2	3	4	5

The Control Scale is probably best used as an individual checklist rather than being interpreted on the basis of an overall score. Most people find that some items do not apply to them, but it is valuable to note the trend in the responses to those questions that are personally relevant. If these answers are typically rated lower than three on the scale, it is likely that lack of control adds to the risk of work-family conflict. You would be an ideal candidate for a family-friendly work environment, and a trip to the company's suggestion box might be in order.

Tailoring the Design

Much of what happens at the workplace is, of course, in the employer's hands. As a result, redesigning work requires ongoing discussion involving management and staff. There are so many factors to consider, such as the size of the organization, the nature of its business, the existing resources in the community, the age of the employees, and their gender and marital status. It is not surprising, therefore, to find that the results of outcome studies are inconsistent; a particular program that proves popular in one organization may receive a failing grade in another. Older employees are likely to be interested in assistance with elder care, for example, while maternity and paternity leave and child care will be more salient issues for a younger group. Day care may be a very attractive option for some employees, but not those with a long commute. (Traveling with young children has been known to take years off a person's life expectancy and may not be a parent's preferred way of starting the day or unwinding from work.)

The ready solution is to ask employees what they want. This type of "needs assessment" is an excellent starting point for two reasons. The first is that it yields valuable information—employees know what would make their lives easier and will be more than happy to share this knowledge with the powers that be. The second is that it creates the optimal atmosphere for change; management is working with staff—not implementing change unilaterally. However, one study of organizations that together employed more than one million people reported that only 5 percent had ascertained employees' family and personal responsibilities.

Staff surveys, focus groups, interviews, and consultation can all contribute to a needs assessment that precedes change. Although the research is scant, gender differences have emerged. Duxbury found that employed mothers had a somewhat different wish list than fathers. For the mothers, flexible work hours were the number-one choice, followed by increased family leave, on-site day care, supervisor understanding, shorter hours, telecommuting, and job-sharing. Men were most enthusiastic about telecommuting, with flexible hours a close second. Supervisor understanding, on-site day care, increased family leave, and shorter hours were the next most frequent items on their list.

The Corporate Culture

A thorough assessment can also identify the concerns that supervisors and others in managerial positions may have. On paper, a policy could reach new heights of family-friendliness, but if your supervisor is anything but friendly as a result, life may not get much better. I read of a simple, but popular, policy introduced by a small company that could not fund expensive options such as subsidized dependent care. Employees were allowed to take vacation days with only a half-hour's notice, which made it easy to be at home when a temporary problem such as a child's illness arose. Such an option might not be exercised, however, if employees expected to be greeted with obvious displeasure from their supervisor. Implementing change is much easier when possible sources of resistance are understood. Educating management as to the benefits of creating a more family-friendly work environment, together with training them how to support their staff, are probably key, but often neglected, factors determining outcome.

The critical issue is one of attitude. Policies are written and programs are established; attitude, however, is shaped. The leadership of the organization is pivotal. Family-friendly practices must be an organizational goal, rather than a concession to keep the masses from rebelling. Companies can now compete for awards given to the most innovative and progressive ideas and practices in this area of human resources. Their desire to do so attests to the willingness of management to give priority to reducing the conflict between work and home.

Sometimes the little touches seem the most indicative of the changes in corporate culture. I once needed to reach a client to cancel an appointment. Realizing he worked on the line at a large car plant led me to assume that my chances of reaching him were slim. To the contrary—the woman answering the phone seemed very agreeable about tracking him down for me. I commented on this when I was speaking to him; it turned out that the company's policy was that all employees were to have ready access to a telephone for personal reasons. It was assumed that people would not abuse this privilege, and apparently there had been little to suggest they did.

Having reserved parking for pregnant employees, allocating rest areas for those who need a nap, providing expectant fathers with "birth alert" beepers, designating a lactation room for nursing mothers, and asking employees to rate management on the degree of sensitivity to work-family issues are small but significant steps. I especially like the idea of stocking the cafeteria with nutritious, reasonably priced, easy-to-heat-up family meals that can be picked up as you head home. All of these measures communicate an understanding that it is no longer reasonable to expect employees to maintain the distinction between work and home that existed in the past. A work environment is created in which the goals of the organization and the needs of its employees are integrated. They do not have to compete with one another; work can be redesigned to everyone's benefit.

Conclusion: The Resilient Family

One of the shortcomings of the mental health field is its emphasis on what is wrong rather than what is right. We are trained to look for, diagnose, and treat problems according to the disease model borrowed from traditional medicine. Not that the model is without merit—I would not be too impressed if I went to hospital with a broken arm only to hear the doctor emphasize that three of my limbs were just fine. The limitation of the disease model, however, is that it tells us very little about why people *don't* get sick. Interest in this question is behind the push towards a more preventative approach in medicine: once you know what keeps people well, let others in on the secret so they too can avoid becoming sick.

The concept of resilience as applied to family life is based on the same principle. It refers to characteristics that allow families to remain strong and adapt successfully to the demands and stresses of an ever-changing world. In spite of the diversity in the findings, certain areas of consistency have emerged that add to our understanding of why the family has never lost its status as the cornerstone of our society.

Problem-Solving

Apart from helping me survive my midlife crisis, my experiences at Outward Bound provided the best definition of a problem I have encountered. My leader turned out to be an ex-student. Shortly after arriving at the wilderness camp, we all headed off for our first attempt at rock-climbing. As we were getting roped up, I noticed he was scrutinizing me. He enquired if I had taught social psychology as he was sure I had been his professor many years before. I confessed that I was probably the person in question and, realizing that he would be holding onto the other end of the rope, asked if I had given him a good mark. "You'll find out," he replied in a playful but ominous tone. I assume that he at least passed as he kept me safe throughout our two weeks together. I also suspect he taught me far more of value than I did when he was my student. I particularly remember the briefing before we headed out on a five-day canoe trip. We would be traveling without any leaders; although they would follow behind, we were on our own and would have to fend for ourselves if problems arose. He emphasized that our initial reaction to a problem was more critical than the nature of the problem itself. He explained that we would have a choice. We could either think of the problem as an obstacle—a barrier to success—or as an opportunity to do something different. From this perspective, "we don't know what to do" would be replaced with "what can we do that we haven't tried yet?"

I am not sure that I would have seen the significance if it had not been of relevance so quickly. Getting lost after taking the wrong portage, being "marooned" on a minuscule island during a storm, having to decide what to do when a canoe was blown loose, and realizing that we had an ample supply of dried, uncooked food, but no dry firewood were just samples of the challenges we faced. I like to think we proved ourselves reasonably resilient—at least we survived to tell the tale.

This view of problems as starting points and opportunities lies at the heart of resilience. The research in this area has encompassed many of the challenges families can face, such as poverty, chronic illness, traumatic injury, separation and divorce, and learning disabilities. As much as the issues may differ, the resilient family's initial response is the same. It involves a search for what can be done to improve the situation rather than an assumption of defeat. This approach also applies to the issues facing families when they experience the conflict and stress that can arise when trying to balance work and home. Such problems need to motivate change—be it improving time management, learning to take better care of ourselves, fine-tuning our parenting style, or talking to our employer about family-friendly initiatives.

Be Informed

Assumptions should be replaced with knowledge. The view that day care is harmful to children was popular, but it was wrong. Assumptions that women were less capable of becoming educated and skilled members of the workforce were also popular and unfounded. The errors have not been trivial; they have generated guilt and added unnecessarily to the conflict between work and home.

Resilient families are well-informed. This does not imply knowing what the solutions are; in fact, part of being well-informed can be the realization that very little is known about a particular issue. Returning to the topic of day care, being well-informed twenty years ago would have meant acknowledging that no one understood the effects of early separation from mothers.

I like to suggest that parents think of themselves as consumers when it comes to advice regarding family life. It is not unusual to want to know as much as possible about the items we are considering for purchase. Comparison shopping is the norm, and we expect manufacturers and salespeople to be able to justify why we should spend our money on their products. It seems less commonplace, however, to insist that experts in the social sciences provide comparable assurances of quality.

As a framework for screening advice, I would like to unveil my Consumer Beware Checklist. This is the result of absolutely no research and to date has been endorsed only by the Flat Earth Society.

The Consumer Beware Checklist

1. Before you read any book about family life, make sure you are feeling calm, relaxed, and good about yourself. If you begin to become anxious and worried by the end of Chapter 1, entertain the suspicion that the author is selling his ideas by playing on parents' number-one soft spot—guilt. If by the end of Chapter 2 you are convinced that you have failed your children miserably, stop reading and send the book immediately to someone you know who always seems so accomplished, superior, and smug about his wonderful family life.

2. Distrust anyone who claims to have "proof" but has neglected to provide details. There is nothing wrong with speculation, and an educated guess can even be enough to win a Nobel Prize. The Nobel laureate in theoretical physics, however, will have maintained a clear distinction between what is known and what is speculated. Expect nothing else from your "expert."

3. Remain unimpressed when the expert tells you she has the support of others in the field. Telltale phrases include "most experts agree" and "experts have known for years that..." There are two points to consider. The first is the question of how the author knows so much about what others in the field believe. The second is that, even if most of them do agree, who's to say it isn't just another example of collective ignorance and misunderstanding?

4. Look out for "runaway reasoning." If the expert begins by discussing employment trends but ends up telling you about the imminent destruction of the world as we know it, recognize that we all get carried away sometimes.

5. Be encouraged by signs that the expert admits he doesn't have a clue. Of course, if each page is full of such confessions, perhaps it was premature for him to go public. The job of experts

and commentators, however, is often to raise questions and *suggest* answers rather make pronouncements.

6. Expect to find mention of alternative viewpoints. When you can tell that the expert has gone through a process of weighing the advantages and disadvantages of different ways of viewing a particular question, there is a good chance she doesn't believe she has a hot line to the truth.

7. Do not be automatically impressed by the number of degrees the person has. In order to get a license to feel the bumps on people's heads, Victorians had to spend many years in graduate school.

I do not want to create an atmosphere of paranoia by suggesting that most people in the social sciences cannot be trusted. Nonetheless, parents should endeavor to make sure that experts are providing valid information rather than personal opinion.

Keep Talking

The importance of communication surfaces in almost all studies of family resilience. The simple reason is that, although it's human nature to want to associate with other people, it is remarkably difficult to do so successfully. Peace and harmony may be goals, but their attainability is an entirely different matter. The discussion of stress in Chapter 1 included a description of what can happen when people keep feelings of frustration and resentment to themselves. Ignoring gender issues relating to child care and housework can transform marriage from a partnership to a battleground. Similarly, not talking about the need to share responsibilities for elder care can permanently damage family relationships.

Talking about matters does not, of course, guarantee that a solution will be forthcoming. I was once part of lengthy discussions about working conditions at a hospital. As far as I was concerned, we presented compelling statistics, brilliant arguments, and heart-wrenching appeals for concessions. Management may have listened, but not one of their hearts was warmed, let alone wrenched. Nothing changed, but at least our concerns had been voiced.

The goal of communication is to create an environment in which people feel they can express their ideas, complaints, and suggestions freely. It is an essential part of maintaining effective relationships, both within families and with the people at work. It may prove to be only the beginning of a lengthy process but is nonetheless an essential first step.

With a Little Help from Our Friends

Not long ago I interviewed a young woman, Sarah, who was applying for custody of her six-year-old brother, Michael. He had come to live with her because of the chronic alcoholism, neglect, and lack of supervision in his parents' home. The court was anticipating that his parents would never be able to make the changes needed to care for him adequately. It was also assumed that Sarah would not be able to provide a stable home; she was only nineteen and had lived in the same environment as her brother for most of her life. The possibility of permanent foster care was being considered, but Sarah stood her ground and remained adamant that Michael continue to live with her. What surprised me was how normal and healthy their new family life appeared to be. In spite of the fact that she had been in the same environment, had an older brother who was in jail, and had an older sister fighting to keep custody of her own child, Sarah had graduated from high school, found a steady job, and built a stable relationship with her boyfriend. Michael was progressing very well at school, and there were signs that he was overcoming the developmental delays that often accompany a history of neglect.

I was impressed by Sarah's resilience. I asked her what made the difference; how she was able to establish what was, in effect, a successful single-parent family while her family of origin had been so disturbed. After thinking for a moment, she began talking about the support she received from others. She had a favorite aunt who was always encouraging her and would provide advice when asked. The friendships she had formed at work were also very important to her, as was her continuing contact with a high school teacher who had taken her under her wing. These people served as her "anchor" or support system, and gave her a sense of security and confidence. The teacher had also inspired Sarah to become a Big Sister. She was now someone else's anchor, and this experience added to how connected she felt to the community.

Sarah's account of her history and family life illustrates the extensive research highlighting the role of support systems in fostering resilience. Strong families are connected at many levels. They derive support from work and are involved in their children's education. They are likely to seek assistance when they have a child with special needs, becoming active in support groups. They endeavor to maintain ties with friends and extended family, and are members of religious denominations, service organizations, and leisure groups that put them in regular contact with others.

It is because of this resilience that the family will continue to evolve. In keeping with my proclaimed inadequacy as a soothsayer, I will not even attempt to predict how the relationship between work and home will change in the future. I remain confident, however, that families do have the resilience needed to adjust to change—and to balance the demands of work and home so that our two most important jobs can combine to give us a rewarding life.

Suggested Reading

The Family Squeeze: Surviving the Sandwich Generation. Suzanne Kingsmill and Benjamin Schlesinger, University of Toronto Press, 1998.

Healthy Together: A Couple's Guide to Midlife Wellness. Christine Langlois, McGraw Hill, 2000.

The Hurried Child: Growing Up Too Fast Too Soon. David Elkind, Addison-Wesley, 1989.

kids are worth it! Giving Your Child the Gift of Inner Discipline. Barbara Coloroso, Penguin Books, 1999.

Learn to Relax: Proven Techniques for Reducing Stress, Tension, and Anxiety—and Promoting Peak Performance. C. Eugene Walker, John Wiley and Sons, 2000.

The Man Who Mistook His Job for a Life: A Chronic Overachiever Finds His Way Home. Jonathon Lezear, Crown Publishers, 2001.

Mind Over Mood: Change How You Feel by Changing the Way You Think. Dennis Greenberger and Christine Padesky, Guildford Press, 1995.

Now I Know Why Tigers Eat Their Young: Surviving a New Generation of Teenagers. Peter Marshall, Whitecap, 2000.

Simplify Your Life: 100 Ways to Slow Down and Enjoy the Things That Really Matter. Elaine St. James, Hyperion, 1994.

Time Management from the Inside Out: The Foolproof System for Taking Control of Your Schedule—and Your Life. Julie Morgenstern, Henry Holt and Co., 2000.

Values Shift: The New Work Ethic and What It Means for Business. John Izzo and Pam Withers, Prentice Hall, 2000.

Your Guide to Caring for Your Aging Parents. Coles Notes, Coles Publishing, 2001.

Index

186